Software Vulnerability Discovery Process: Concepts and Applications

RIVER PUBLISHERS SERIES IN MATHEMATICAL, STATISTICAL AND COMPUTATIONAL MODELLING FOR ENGINEERING

Applied mathematical techniques along with statistical and computational data analysis has become vital skills across the physical sciences. The purpose of this book series is to present novel applications of numerical and computational modelling and data analysis across the applied sciences. We encourage applied mathematicians, statisticians, data scientists and computing engineers working in a comprehensive range of research fields to showcase different techniques and skills, such as differential equations, finite element method, algorithms, discrete mathematics, numerical simulation, machine learning, probability and statistics, fuzzy theory, etc.

Books published in the series include professional research monographs, edited volumes, conference proceedings, handbooks and textbooks, which provide new insights for researchers, specialists in industry, and graduate students.

Topics included in this series are as follows:

- Discrete mathematics and computation
- Fault diagnosis and fault tolerance
- Finite element method (FEM) modeling/simulation
- Fuzzy and possibility theory
- Fuzzy logic and neuro-fuzzy systems for relevant engineering applications
- Game Theory
- Mathematical concepts and applications
- Modelling in engineering applications
- Numerical simulations
- Optimization and algorithms
- Queueing systems
- Resilience
- Stochastic modelling and statistical inference
- Stochastic Processes
- Structural Mechanics
- Theoretical and applied mechanics

For a list of other books in this series, visit www.riverpublishers.com

Software Vulnerability Discovery Process: Concepts and Applications

Adarsh Anand

Department of Operational Research, University of Delhi
Delhi, India

Navneet Bhatt

Anil Surendra Modi School of Commerce, SVKM's Narsee Monjee Institute of Management Studies (NMIMS), Mumbai, India

Omar H Alhazmi

Department of Computer Science, Taibah University, Medina, Saudi Arabia

River Publishers

Routledge
Taylor & Francis Group
NEW YORK AND LONDON

Published 2025 by River Publishers
River Publishers
Alsbjergvej 10, 9260 Gistrup, Denmark
www.riverpublishers.com

Distributed exclusively by Routledge
605 Third Avenue, New York, NY 10017, USA
4 Park Square, Milton Park, Abingdon, Oxon OX14 4RN

Software Vulnerability Discovery Process: Concepts and Applications / by Adarsh Anand, Navneet Bhatt, Omar H Alhazmi.

Routledge is an imprint of the Taylor & Francis Group, an informa business

ISBN 978-87-7022-862-6 (hardback)
ISBN 978-87-7004-780-7 (paperback)
ISBN 978-87-7004-618-3 (online)
ISBN 978-87-7004-617-6 (master ebook)

Dr. Adarsh Anand would like to dedicate this book to his loving daughters; Ahana & Aavya

Dr. Navneet Bhatt would like to dedicate this book to his loving parents and wife

Prof (Dr) Omar Alhazmi would like to dedicate this book to his parents and family for their continuous support

Contents

Preface

With the inception of advancements in the computing technologies, the reliability of the systems has increased manifolds. The proliferation of technologies has gone far beyond even the most optimistic forecasts. By virtue of ongoing advances in networking, internet has now become a necessity. But, like it is said, every coin has two sides; this exhaustive connectivity of computing systems has further raised the already existing security concerns in the software world. It is of late that researchers have developed interest in investigating potential number of vulnerabilities by making use of quantitative models. Vulnerabilities have been reported in various software systems and in order to mitigate the risk associated with these vulnerabilities, both the developers and the users have to utilize resources.

This textbook *Software Vulnerability Discovery Process: Concepts and Applications* is a part of book series *Mathematical, Statistical and Computational Modelling for Engineering Sciences* and includes several analytically described existing models and their concepts explained in a layman manner so as to make it easily understandable.

This book is designed to understand the use of basic fundamentals, various mathematical models, and approaches that illustrate the analytical reasoning and modeling that can provide an in-depth understanding of the thin line of difference and that minute connectivity of the software vulnerability models with the already available concepts of software reliability growth modeling. In the chapters, focus has been on to explain the concepts utilized by various researchers so as to understand the software vulnerability discovery process from a conceptual framework. Some chapters also carry the numerical illustration part to showcase the application of the discussed models.

It is our hope that academicians who wish to enhance their knowledge regarding the concepts of software vulnerability discovery process will find this book useful as a reference guide and to practitioners who seek to apply these available quantification models. In general, we hope that the readers find it useful for better understanding of the mathematics behind these ever evolving models.

Adarsh Anand
Department of Operational Research, University of Delhi,
Delhi 110007, India
adarsh.anand86@gmail.com

Navneet Bhatt
Anil Surendra Modi School of Commerce, SVKM's Narsee Monjee Institute of Management Studies (NMIMS), Mumbai 400056, India
navneetbhatt@live.com

Omar H. Alhazmi
Department of Computer Science, Taibah University, Medina, Saudi Arabia
ohhazmi@taibahu.edu.sa

Acknowledgement

The authors are grateful to various colleagues both in academia and industry who read through draft manuscripts. Gratitude also goes to Chanchal, Asha Yadav, and Divya, research scholars at Department of Operational Research, University of Delhi, India, who have helped in carrying out the reading of the drafts as and when needed. Special thanks to Garima Babbar, another scholar at the Department of Operational Research, who has worked tirelessly and helped finalizing the layout of the work. Our appreciation also goes out to *Rajiv Prasad*, from River Publishers, who has played a vital role in letting us know guidelines and other steps of the manuscript production process. In addition, we are honored to be associated with Prof. Mangey Ram, who showed faith in us for carrying out the book compilation work under his series.

Of course, no author can successfully complete a book project without the support of family. Our beloved appreciation to our respective families for affording us their patience so that our thought could be translated and compiled in the form of this book.

Adarsh Anand
Navneet Bhatt
Omar H. Alhazmi

List of Figures

List of Tables

List of Abbreviations

AIC	Akaike information criterion
AME	Alhazmi and Malaiya effort
AML	Alhazmi and Malaiya logistic
CDF	Cumulative distribution function
CERT	Computer Emergency Response Team
CSRF	Cross-site Request Forgery
CVEs	Common vulnerabilities and exposures
CVSS	Common vulnerability scoring system
CWE	Common weakness enumeration
CWSS	Common weakness scoring system
DoS	Denial of service
HTTP	Hypertext transfer protocol
ID	Identifier
KLOC	Kilo lines of code
LOC	Line of code
MEOP	Mean error of prediction
MFSA	Mozilla Firefox security advisory
MLE	Maximum likelihood estimation
MS	Microsoft Security Bulletin
MSE	Mean squared error
MTBF	Mean time between failure
MTTNV	Mean time to next failure
MTTNV	Mean time until the next vulnerability
MVDM	Multiple-version software vulnerability discovery approach
NHPP	Non-homogeneous Poisson process
NIST	National Institute of Standards and Technology
NLLS	Non-linear least square
NVD	National Vulnerability Database
PDF	Probability density function
PE	Prediction error

PRR	Prediction-ratio risk
RMSPE	Root mean square prediction error
SDLC	Software development life cycle
SQL	Structured query language
SRE	Software reliability engineering
SRGM	Software reliability growth model
SRM	Software reliability model
SSRF	Server-Side Request Forgery
TS	Theil statistics
VDM	Vulnerability discovery model
VPM	Vulnerability patch modeling
XSS	Cross-site scripting

1

Introduction

The way software engineering is done now differs significantly from ten or twenty years ago. Computers were like islands unto themselves when there was little or no network access. Typically, software applications were evaluated for functionality on isolated systems before being released as independent units. There was no market for software services at the time other than in idea. Since the worst that might happen after a breach was that the exploit could only attack them in a confined environment, security was not regarded as a crucial factor. However, the expansion of the Internet and technological advancements caused a swift paradigm shift in the way computer systems are networked and the beginning of the development of software applications, having a significant impact on security. Because of the present society's high level of computer and network connectivity, applications that are not designed to function securely are increasingly vulnerable to attack from both insiders and outsiders.

Software security, in the context of the software development process, is a continuing process that ensures the integrity, confidentiality, and reliability of a software system by incorporating various practices to maintain an application. A software developer always strives to create secure software by utilizing a process that is inspired by security. The majority of software has flaws that developers may have unintentionally or intentionally introduced during the software development process. Two fundamental problems – complexity and incentive – can be linked to the prevalence of bugs. As technology develops, it becomes increasingly important for software developers to provide products that are more sophisticated, and application development security typically becomes more difficult. The second issue with security is a lack of motivation: most software developers are adept at developing secure usage environments, but due to the economics of the software industry, they are provided with little incentive. Our failure to gauge software security is a contributing factor in the development of both of these issues. We can define *software security* as a system's ability to carry out its essential tasks without violating its explicit or implicit security policy breaches due to software. Software security, to put it more colloquially, is the degree to which software is free of bugs of certain types.

Let us now examine the scope of software security more closely.

1.1 What is Software Security?

The question of "what is security?" is a common one, and it refers to the idea of incorporating safeguards into the building of software to enable it stay operational (or attack-resistant). In order to determine a piece of software's resistance to malicious attacks, it must pass software security testing before being released on the market.

Everyone has their own concept of security. Even for the same person, its meaning can vary with the circumstances. We view security as imposing a policy that specifies the terms under which resources may be accessed. There is a security breach if we do not want unapproved users accessing our system but they are. Denial-of-service attacks are also likely to be in violation of our terms of service about the required level of availability for our system or servers. We may sometimes get by without a formalized security policy because the implicit security policies one is so generally accepted. When there is not a clear policy in place, however, determining whether or not an occurrence constitutes a security breach can become argumentative. Can we say that in a multi-user system, a user who accesses the personal information of another user is not violating the security system? Do port scans count as security breaches? Should you take precautions against such "attacks"? A user's reading of another's private information does not compromise the system's safety. In spite of this fact, we think there is a flaw in the development of the system. Addressing this issue may require shifting emphasis from the security system itself to the security policy. If we are concerned about security, it is not because we cannot agree on whether or not a given activity constitutes a threat. Rather, we are concerned about whether or not the consequences will be serious, and whether or not we can do something to address the possible issue.

1.2 The Importance of Software Security Metrics

It is true that there are numerous criteria for gauging software security, but none of them provide a full picture. It is difficult to measure the complexity of software; however, factors like software size and complexity can provide a rough approximation of the number of vulnerabilities inherent in a given piece of software. Both the number of defects per line of code (LOC) and the number of defects discovered in a given time period can be quantified; however, the former depends in part on the product's popularity with users or the intensity of its usage, and the latter is only practical after the product has been in circulation for some time. Finally, the amount of effort put into security during software design and implementation could be evaluated, but this does not guarantee successful outcomes.

It should come as no surprise that security metrics are crucial in the field of software engineering, since we cannot reliably improve upon what we cannot measure. There is a never-ending supply of new development processes and technologies aimed at software engineers, all of which claim to enhance product security and stability. Software developers must keep up with the ever-evolving set of resources and methodologies that ensures a safe and dependable end result. It is challenging to decide on a set of tools and technologies without some sort of security metric. Motivations to take security metrics into account during software development are needed in the software business. Consumers are more likely to choose cutting-edge, first-to-market software if those criteria are met. Flaws in software's security, malware, and worms are all possible outcomes. However, it has been observed that software companies are deterred from investing in security because customers have no interest in paying more for a safer product.

If we look at asymmetric information theory (Akerlof, 1978), we can understand why software companies are not investing more in security. Let us pretend there is a city where there are 100 reliable secondhand automobiles ("plums") and 100 duds (often known as "lemons"). It is worth $3000 for the plums and $1000 for the lemons. However, only vendors are aware of whether or not they are offering quality automobiles; customers have no way of knowing it. If customers believe their chances of receiving a plum are equivalent to those of receiving a lemon, then the market price will begin at $2000. However, at that price, only lemons will be offered for sale. Buyers are reluctant to pay more than $1000 since they might be getting a lemon, so this market clearing price may come as a surprise. However, at that price, no owner of a nice car will sell it; as a result, only lemons are offered for sale. To rephrase, there will be significant downward pressure on price and quality when purchasers do not have as much knowledge as sellers do about the quality of the products. This is a common complaint among those in the information security industry across a variety of product and component distribution channels. Even if sellers have a gut feeling about the safety of their software, there is no reason for customers to believe a vendor's claims about the safety of their products. Since there is no incentive for either the buyer or the seller to invest in security, neither is willing to do so (Anderson, 2001).

The "market for lemons" effect could be mitigated if there was a reliable way to gauge software security, which would reduce information asymmetry.

1.3 Software Security Metrics: What Can We Measure?

A metric is a numerical representation of the extent to which a system, part, or procedure has a certain characteristic. To quantify anything, one compares it to some kind of benchmark. We can define software security metric as a set of interrelated dimensions (measured against a benchmark) that allows for the quantification of the degree to which one is protected from the risk of loss or harm due to an attack."

The security metrics are context sensitive and environment dependent. Depending on the situation, the score of a metric may be interpreted in different ways. For example, if we say that in our system, we have 250,000 vulnerabilities; although this seems like a huge number, we cannot be certain of it. Let us do some joint analysis by posing some questions and considering some scenarios. We have a major problem if we have six servers. The situation improves if we have 3000 servers available. It is a different story if 95% of those flaws are critical as opposed to 5%. Just where are these flaws in the software component? Have they been spotted on our most important component? In many cases, we fail to give necessary context. The security rating and scores will differ, potentially significantly, in different organizations and business environments, based on the type of software we are into.

Metrics need the inclusion of a time component in the measurement. More so, if a company has a security problem, a single metric will not fix it. Understanding the metric's intended use requires some serious reflection. The challenge is in the creation of security metrics that are not overly complex but still give decision-makers actionable data that is directly tied to their security goals. The measurements should serve to educate the business by revealing areas of improvement. A security metric, by definition, must involve some sort of counting or measuring. But in what ways can we quantify these claims? How can we quantify security? We may list out some traditional metrics that could be used to measure the security of a software.

- *Size and complexity*: Metrics concerned with size typically express themselves in terms of the number of lines of code written in the software, or kilo lines of code (KLOC). The complexity of a software is a way of describing its unique qualities. These traits are concerned with the way your code communicates with others. All of these features add up to your code's complexity.

- *Number of flaws detected over time*: It evaluates the effectiveness of observing security occurrences. However, it does not consider the points at which an event or investigation is initiated. Nor it considers their reasons of detection.
- *Cost per defect*: This metric is designed to calculate the actual business loss caused by security flaws.
- *Number of attack surface*: It calculates how many points of entry exist in a system and how likely each is to be exploited by an attacker.
- *Cost of security breaches*: It quantify the actual financial harm to a company caused by security breaches.

When it comes to measuring the efficacy of an organization's security program, it is important to evaluate the efficacy of recent security-related expenditures.

1.4 Security: Isn't That Just Reliability?

It is logical to make a comparison between reliability and security. We may say that there is a strong relationship between reliability and security. A software's reliability can be thought of as a gauge of how well it handles a variety of potential bugs. A bug's definition can be thought of as a security policy in reverse. We can think of security as a metric for gauging the reliability of your software program in light of a given security standard. Some contend that security is a special case of reliability, while others maintain the opposite. As far as we are concerned, security is just another aspect of reliability. An issue exists if it is possible to bypass some sort of security measure.

While it is true that reliability issues are not necessarily security issues, it is important to keep in mind that this is not always the case. Some bugs, such as those that cause a software to crash, could allow an attacker to get access to protected data. However, issues with reliability are often the same as denial-of-service attacks. A denial-of-service attack can be launched against the website if an attacker discovers and exploits a "crasher" in the web server we are using. In most cases, the security of the software can be enhanced if we employ good software reliability strategies, especially in the face of certain types of attacks. If we are concerned about the security of the product, we should also make it more reliable.

As we have said that, software reliability issues can be due to any type of software bugs. The purpose of reliability testing is to find bugs in the software's design and functionality by simulating real-world usage in controlled conditions. As a subset of software testing, it is the process of establishing whether or not the software can run without crashing for a predetermined amount of time in a controlled setting. The process verifies that the item functions properly and can be relied upon for its intended use. Software reliability is an important part of software development life cycle (SDLC); in this book, we will not be discussing that kind of content. But, as far as the security bugs are concerned, those can be considered as a subset of reliability bugs. And hence a proper widely accepted, standard definition is required. In the next section, we discuss the software reliability engineering and related bugs and anomalies.

1.5 Software Reliability Engineering

A software's security can be improved by learning about the types of hidden flaws it contains and how they are typically uncovered. As we have already discussed, security flaws fall under the broader category of reliability flaws, and the majority of flaws are the result of poor work throughout the development phase of software.

The goal of software reliability engineering is to reduce the number and severity of implementation errors. Therefore, software security and reliability engineering go hand in hand. Software engineering is a systematic application of computer engineering approach that benefits from standardized terminology. In the "IEEE Standard Glossary of Software Engineering Terminology" document, software engineering is defined as "The application of a systematic, disciplined, quantifiable approach to the development, operation, and maintenance of software" (IEEE, 1990). Methods based on quantitative measures of reliability are used in software reliability engineering (SRE) to make this evaluation. Estimation, prediction, measurement, and modeling are only few of the quantitative methods used in SRE. Quantitatively characterizing how software is utilized is fundamental to SRE because product and service dependability is heavily influenced by operating conditions, and software reliability is related to how software is used (Everett et al., 2002).

The software development life cycle (SDLC) models that are currently in use are well-founded process models of SRE that explain the various phases of software development in a sequential and planned manner. The software development life cycle (SDLC) is often represented by the following stages in most models: requirement analysis and definition; system design; program design; coding; testing; delivery; and maintenance. Throughout the software development life cycle (SDLC), the SRE toolkit equips the developer with the means to monitor, control, and ultimately boost software quality. Software reliability models have been created to take SRE into a quantitative realm. In this book, we will not explore that kind of content. Some excellent books have been written on the subject of software testing and reliability, including two classics, *The Handbook of Software Reliability Engineering* by Michael R. Lyu (Lyu, 1996) and *Software Reliability* by Hoang Pham (Pham, 2000).

1.6 Software Security Engineering

Software security engineering's integration into the SDLC yields numerous advantages, including the enhanced capacity to detect and repair security-related flaws and the broadened participation of the ecosystem in resolving security-related issues. The goal of security engineering is to create systems that can withstand intrusion, human error, and other forms of malicious activity. The major focus that remains here is about the security-related bugs and their discovery, disclosure, fixing, publication, and automation of the exploitation.

We can define security engineering as adding and enforcing security measures in the software infrastructure such that they become an intrinsic element of a firm's operational capability. Under this, security is considered at every stage of the software development life cycle (SDLC) and everyone involved is held responsible for the system's safety. The design, development, implementation, and execution of technical controls are all part of security engineering services. The increasing threat of cyberattacks highlights the need for businesses to employ software engineering services to guarantee bug-free code that can resist any attack. This safeguards the interests of the business, its clients, and its customers.

At various points in the development process, the software's reliability is evaluated so that informed choices can be made. It is important to distinguish between various types of software bugs found during the testing and operational phase of a software.

1.7 Software Bugs and Anomalies

As said by the late computer scientist Edsger W. Dijkstra:

> If debugging is the process of removing software bugs, then programming must be the process of putting them in

Programming mistakes of all shapes and sizes are frequently encountered during the software development process. The various implementation mistakes done during the software development process can be organized into various types to make triage decisions as per the "IEEE Standard Glossary of Software Engineering Terminology" document (IEEE, 1990).

- **Failure**: A failure in a software is defined as "the inability of a system or component to perform its required functions within specified performance requirement."
- **Fault**: A fault is "an incorrect step, process, or data definition in a computer program."
- **Mistake**: A mistake is "a human action that produces an incorrect result."
- **Error**: An error is defined as "the difference between a computed, observed, or measured value or condition and the true, specified, or theoretically correct value or condition."

The flaws in the software are what lead to the failures. However, not all mistakes always result in failure. Software *bugs* (an informal name specified for *defect*), on the other hand, might be failures, faults, or errors. Software testers typically use this term to refer to any mistake, defect, or flaw discovered while using a piece of software.

1.7.1 Defects

A defect is majorly classified based on its severity and priority. The level of a defect's destructive influence on the software requirements specification determines the defect's severity. Table 1.1 provides the classification of defects based on priority and severity. The types of defect severity that are frequently used in software development include the following:

Table 1.1 Classification of defects based on priority and severity.

Based on priority	Based on the severity
Immediate/critical	Critical
High	Major
Medium	Minor
Low	Trivial

- **Critical**: A defect that entirely prevents the software from executing a key feature or functionality. For example: If a user forgot password in any login interface, the user is prompted to enter the OTP they received through email or their registered mobile number. A loader is displayed after entering the OTP, and it keeps on indefinitely. It is a critical defect that the user cannot log in to use the application's functionalities.
- **Major**: A defect that causes a major functionality or feature to act significantly differently from how it is described in the software's requirements specification. For example: In a login interface, when the system accepts the entered username as authorization to access the platform without verifying the associated account's password. Because of this, an unauthorized user may access the account, which is a major defect that could result in the theft of private data.
- **Minor**: A defect that affects only a capability or feature slightly, such as when it behaves differently from how it should or displays some other odd behavior. For example: After entering the username and password, the user successfully logs into his or her account, but a popup window with the message "Login Unsuccessful Please Try Again Later" is displayed in its place. As it simply presented with the incorrect prompt box, this is a minor defect.
- **Trivial**: Any aesthetic flaws, such as out-of-place photos, misspelt words, alignment problems, or incorrect font casing, are categorized as trivial defects. For example: In a login interface, the username and password fields are arranged incorrectly, with the password field coming first.

A defect priority is cataloging of a defect based on the priority with which it should be rectified. Priority is given to defects that render a software system useless than to a defect that just affects a tiny portion of its usefulness. According to the severity of the fault and business requirements, business stakeholders, the product owner, project managers, and business analysts determine the defect's priority. The defect is classified based on priority as critical, high, medium, and low:

- **Immediate/critical**: A defect that needs to be corrected right away because it seriously affects system and business requirements. It prevents the system from carrying out necessary functions and stops the software's testing from being carried out, rendering the system useless. For example: Suppose an e-commerce website's home page misspells the firm name, which raises the defect's priority to critical but reduces its severity to low. Although misspellings can give consumers the impression that a company's website is fraudulent, which could result in lost sales, wrong spellings do not impair the website's functionality.

- **High**: A high priority defect requires less attention as compared to critical defects but still needs more than other remaining priority groups. Once critical problems are fixed, then these flaws are fixed. A software defect or occasionally an environmental issue that has an impact on business operations and a key capability or feature of software falls under the category of high priority. For example, whenever we add an item to the cart of an e-commerce shopping website, it crashes.
- **Medium**: A defect with medium severity does not urgently need to be corrected because it will not significantly affect business operations or functionality. These defects are corrected once the immediate and high priority flaws have been addressed. This category includes all minor severity defects. For example, if we buy something on an e-commerce website. The website's cart now includes the purchased item, but the payment portal displays "Payment Unsuccessful" prompt after making a payment.
- **Low**: A flaw that does not significantly affect how software functions and does not require quick remedy. It can be rectified later or when more urgent defects are fixed. This group includes all defects with a low severity category. For example, the navigation bar is not aligned properly on the home screen of a website.

1.7.2 Software security and vulnerabilities

Information security encompasses not just software security but also hardware security, cloud security, Internet of Things security and environmental security, etc. Since additional safeguards, such as a firewall, may mitigate the risk; a single software system's vulnerability might not have a significant impact on the risk an organization faces as a whole. However, the security of software is essential to the overall security of a company and to the effectiveness of whatever security metrics it employs. Systems that are accessible over the Internet provide a greater danger due to the presence of security flaws, as these flaws are virtually always accompanied by malicious activity.

Software vulnerabilities in widely deployed systems are often exploited within days of their public disclosure. For example, in May 2017, WannaCry ransomware encrypted data on machines running the Microsoft Windows operating system and demanded ransom payments in the form of the Bitcoin cryptocurrencies from victims around the world. If a system is infected with one of these worms, it must be fixed immediately, regardless of whether or not it is responsible for safeguarding any critical data. In addition, it is impossible to know in advance which vulnerabilities will be exploited by worms; thus, every system that can be accessed via the Internet should be considered vulnerable.

Furthermore, the security of particular software systems is a part of any risk model a firm creates. Until we have a more reliable method of measuring software security, any numbers we use to assign to its various parts will be little more than an educated guess. That is why it is crucial to have a way to gauge how secure a company's software is. The vulnerability history of a piece of software is one factor that should be taken into account when designing a security solution because it may be helpful in providing information about security. In addition, it offers a wealth of data that may be used to analyze software system behavior in light of patching and exploitability issues.

1.8 Insight into Vulnerabilities

In this book, we have focused on how to examine software security based on vulnerability data that may be retrieved when the product is in use. Over time, vulnerabilities will be uncovered, and when they are, they will be examined from both mathematical and economic perspectives.

The first strategy makes use of what could be called mathematical data. It handles information on vulnerabilities, fixes, exploits, and so on. This strategy makes use of statistical analysis of previously reported vulnerabilities in addition to system features. A second strategy takes into account financial information, such as how vulnerability incentive programs are handled and how resources are allocated for detection. To predict various vulnerability characteristics on systems with the same working environment, the engineering technique uses an examination of a system in which the vulnerabilities have been documented. In addition, systems operating on an open-source platform are more suited to the viability of this strategy. In particular, it will help vendors focus their efforts on the most critical system vulnerabilities. Both of these streams shed light on the types of vulnerabilities in a system, how quickly they are being found and fixed, and how much time and money are needed to find the most severe flaws. These two methods can work together to form a more refined procedure for ensuring the safety of software by organizing the necessary steps for finding vulnerabilities and fixing them.

References

Akerlof, G. A. (1978). The market for "lemons": Quality uncertainty and the market mechanism. In Uncertainty in economics (pp. 235-251). Academic Press.

Anderson, R. (2001, December). Why information security is hard-an economic perspective. In Seventeenth Annual Computer Security Applications Conference (pp. 358-365). IEEE.

IEEE. (1990, December 31). IEEE Standard Glossary of Software Engineering Terminology. Retrieved from https://ieeexplore.ieee.org/document/159342

Everett, W. W., Musa, J. D., Ackerman, A. F., & Wilson, G. A. (2002). Software Reliability Engineering. Encyclopedia of Software Engineering.

Lyu, M. R. (1996). Handbook of Software Reliability Engineering. USA: McGraw-Hill.

Pham, H. (2000). Software reliability. Springer Science & Business Media.

2

Concepts and Definitions

In Chapter 1, we examined the software security and few fundamental metrics accessible to understand it. We noted that there are just a few key distinctions between reliability defects and security bugs. Each type and degree of defect found during software debugging is treated differently. The software engineering approach stresses the production of software through a well-defined set of activities. Security is built in from the start of the software development process. Due to the lack of consensus on a common set of terms for discussing software security, much clarification is needed. Some terminologies have different meanings depending on whether we are looking at them from the intruder's or the defender's perspective, which can lead to a lot of misunderstanding because the perspectives are not usually specified when individuals use the terms. For instance, Arbaugh *et al.* observed that the term "intrusion" can be interpreted differently by the defender and the intruder of a system. An incursion, from the perspective of the attacker, is any action that occurs as a result of the attack. From the perspective of the defender, every unexpected activity that results from a threat to the system is an incursion. Unlike in software engineering, where many terminologies are well established, the computer security sector lacks a universally accepted definition of software vulnerability, making it all the more crucial to define the terms linked to software security.

2.1 Software Vulnerability

It is not always easy to create software. Complicating factors in the software development lifecycle include a rise in problem complexity, design complexity, or program complexity (Conte, 1986). Errors, faults, and failures are introduced in many stages of the software lifecycle (Beizer, 2003). A category of software flaws, known as software vulnerabilities, can have serious effects that go against security protocols. In addition to reducing the system's value or utility, they can also lead to data loss. Since the term "software vulnerability" lacks a universally agreed-upon definition, it is difficult to objectively measure the characteristics of vulnerabilities or to generalize about this class of failures. First, let us define what we mean by "software vulnerability."

2.1.1 Definition

Various researchers and security engineers have presented their own definitions of software vulnerability; however, the majority of these have serious shortcomings. For instance, some definitions of a software vulnerability in a computer system consider that a vulnerability is an outcome of security system violation.

> A weakness in the security system, for example, in procedures, design, or implementation, that might be exploited to cause loss or harm. (Pfleeger & Pfleeger, 2007)

However, there are some cases that we consider to be vulnerabilities that are not taken into account when talking about security systems. Take, as an example, a shared system that stores sensitive information but does not enforce user permissions. There is no security system to violate when a user accesses another's personal information. However, there is a flaw in the design of this system. One way to address this issue is to change the emphasis from the security system to the security policy.

The most widely accepted definition was provided by the "Computer Science and Telecommunications Board of the US National Research Council." It does not, however, take into account whether or not similar fault occurrences should be grouped together as the same vulnerability.

> A weakness in a system that can be exploited to violate the system's intended behavior. (Computer Science and Telecommunications Board, 2001)

Ivan Krsul provided a term that was more concise and it appears that this concept is more applicable in the context of software vulnerability, owing to the fact that it caters to several stages at which a vulnerability could occur, namely the specification, development, and configuration stages, respectively. In addition, the emphasis is placed on the security policy rather than the security system. Ivan Krsul put forward the following definition in his proposal:

> An instance of error in the specification, development, or configuration of software such that its execution can violate the security policy. (Krsul, 1998)

According to the aforementioned definition, the term "error" refers to the defects that were fetched in a variety of stages. Because of this, a vulnerability is an instance of a single weakness or error that is present in a piece of software. In the event when one module contains a vulnerability of a particular type and another module contains a vulnerability of the same type, then this condition is met. According to the criteria presented before, both of these flaws can then be considered to be two distinct flaws in the system. It is reasonable to infer that vulnerabilities are a subset of flaws that have the potential to affect the security policies of a piece of software. This definition classifies vulnerabilities as a subset of defects. Vulnerabilities are the same as flaws; however, flaws are not always vulnerabilities. Both of these words can describe the outcomes of poor design decisions. Vulnerabilities can include not just software flaws but also exposure to hardware tampering, social engineering, and so on.

2.1.2 Terminology

There are many people and organizations involved in software security, all working together to find vulnerabilities. Because of their significance to this piece of work, the following words have been defined.

The instances of security flaws in a software system can be found and reported by *a reporter* or *detector*. A detector notifies the appropriate vendors or disclosure institutions when the occurrence of a vulnerability has occurred. An additional classification for a detector is either benign or malevolent. A benign detector is one that focuses on finding vulnerabilities in order to prevent such vulnerabilities from being exploited. When a vulnerability is discovered, a *benign detector* could send an alert to a disclosure institution or directly to the vendor. They are also referred to as "white hats" in other accounts. A *malevolent detector* will always try to uncover instances of vulnerabilities, with the intention of either selling this information on the black market or using it to exploit a software system. "Black hat" is a word that is sometimes used to refer to malevolent detectors.

A *vendor* is an individual or organization that creates and sells software products or services to consumers or businesses. A security tester working on behalf of a vendor to hunt for vulnerabilities that are expected to be present in a software product is known as a vendor detector. In the context of vulnerabilities, there are public repositories that are used to publicly publish and propagate vulnerability information. Some institutes include the Bugtraq, the Computer Emergency Response Team (CERT), and the Secunia disclosure list. These are only a few examples. A *disclosure institution* is a third-party organization in which a reporter reports vulnerability, which are then forwarded to vendor(s), and a time frame is provided for the vendor(s) to devise a patch that would remedy the vulnerabilities. Some disclosure organizations, such as Bugtraq, often adhere to the practices of immediate and complete disclosure. In contrast, organizations such as CERT provide a window of time that is 45 days long. After that point, the vulnerability in question will be made public, regardless of whether a fix is available or whether there are any workarounds. In the late 1990s, detectors began reporting vulnerabilities to vendors in anticipation of a patch being developed by the vendor. This gave rise to the establishment of disclosure institutions. Patches are frequently delayed, and it is unlikely that vendors would suffer financial loss as a result of exploits in many situations. This led to the introduction of *disclosure procedures*, which stipulate that the vendor or vendors in question must be made aware of the vulnerability before it is made public in order to reduce the risk that is associated with the vulnerability and to give time to create a patch before the detector makes the vulnerability public.

2.1.3 Disclosure policies

As was said earlier, one may categorize a reporter based on the aim they are reporting with. The terms "benign" and "malicious" are at the center of a number of key distinctions that are established throughout the process of vulnerability discovery. For instance, companies could regard detectors to be harmless, provided the detectors in question adhere to a certain vulnerability disclosure policy. Because the many players in the vulnerability lifecycle pursue different aims and adhere to varying beliefs, the meanings of these words have always contained, and will continue to contain, a degree of ambiguity. When we refer to an actor as "benign" in this context, we mean that they adhere to the ideals of "responsible disclosure." Before disclosing a vulnerability to the general public, a detector must comply with the terms of a responsible disclosure policy, which state that the vendor in question must be informed of the flaw and given sufficient time to develop a fix. One policy that demonstrates responsible disclosure is that of CERT/CC, which is as follows:

> Vulnerabilities reported to the CERT/CC will be disclosed to the public 45 days after the initial report, regardless of the existence or availability of patches or workarounds from affected vendors. Extenuating circumstances, such as active exploitation, threats of an especially serious (or trivial) nature, or situations that require changes to an established standard may result in earlier or later disclosure. Disclosures made by the CERT/CC will include credit to the reporter unless otherwise requested by the reporter. We will apprise any affected vendors of our publication plans and negotiate alternate publication schedules with the affected vendors when required.
>
> It is the goal of this policy to balance the need of the public to be informed of security vulnerabilities with vendors' need for time to respond effectively. The final determination of a publication schedule will be based on the best interests of the community overall.
>
> Vulnerabilities reported to us will be forwarded to the affected vendors as soon as practical after we receive the report. The name and contact information of the reporter will be forwarded to the affected vendors unless otherwise requested by the reporter. We will advise the reporter of significant changes in the status of any vulnerability he or she reported to the extent possible without revealing information provided to us in confidence. (CERT, 2019)

If a vulnerability detector makes a vulnerability public without first contacting the vendor and providing the company with sufficient time to produce a fix, then that vulnerability detector is following the practice of *immediate disclosure*.

A guideline is provided by ISO that gives good direction for the disclosure of vulnerabilities in products and services. Disclosure of vulnerabilities assists in the prioritization of risk, improves the protection of systems and data, and enables the prioritization of investments in cybersecurity. Disclosure of vulnerabilities in a coordinated manner is especially vital in situations when many suppliers are impacted. Additionally, ISO publishes guidelines that include criteria and advice for how to process and correct any vulnerabilities. These guidelines may be found on their website (https://www.iso.org/standard/72311.html).

2.1.4 Vulnerability lifecycle

This section will explain a lifecycle that explains the states that a vulnerability can enter over its existence. These states are described here in this part. In spite of the fact that the phrase "lifecycle" suggests a predetermined and orderly transition from one phase to the next, the process of locating and exploiting system vulnerabilities does not always adhere to such a neat pattern. Instead, the advancement is dependent on the interactions between the invading scripts, the programs that exploit the host system's vulnerabilities, and the system itself. There are many cases wherein a vulnerability that is discovered may leapfrog a specific stage.

In general, a vulnerability will go through the following stages: birth, discovery, disclosure, the delivery of a patch, publishing, and the exploit. Intuitively, the number of incursions into computer systems as a consequence of exploiting a particular vulnerability would resemble the graph as shown in Figure 2.1 over the course of time (Arbaugh et.al., 2000).

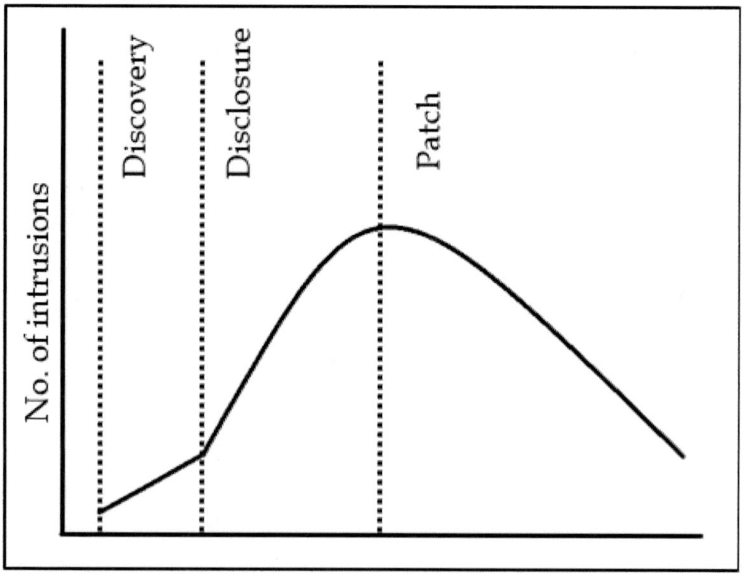

Figure 2.1 Average number of intrusions for a security bug over time (Arbaugh et.al., 2000).

Once a vulnerability has been discovered by the community, it is presumed that the number of incursions will rise, and the rate at which they will increase will quicken as word of the vulnerability spreads to a broader audience. This pattern will continue until the vendor creates a patch or a workaround, at which point the incursion rate will begin to decline. Instead of the gradual fall seen in Figure 2.1, the ideal situation would call for a steeper decline to take place. However, it does take some time for word of the patch to propagate, and much more time for people to actually install it on their systems. In addition, conservative organizations demand testing before making any system modifications, which is a reasonable requirement as testing helps to guarantee that the patch does not cause any new issues. Some companies and organizations will apply the patch as soon as they "get to it," while others may never install it at all for any one of a number of possible reasons.

The lifecycle of a vulnerability may be broken down into a number of distinct stages that can help us understand how vulnerabilities behave. The usual order of appearance of states is as follows:

- **Birth**: Birth is the process by which a defect is created, and it typically takes place accidentally throughout the process of developing a huge project. Discovery and birth both take place at the same time if the birth was malicious and hence purposeful. By convention, we do not consider the vulnerability to exist until there is a nonzero likelihood that it will be deployed; only deployment counts. It is also called injection date.
- **Discovery**: The flaw is referred to be a vulnerability after it has been determined that a product poses a risk to the user's safety or capacity to survive. It makes no difference whether the discoverer had malevolent (Black Hat) or benign (White Hat) intentions when they made their discovery. It is very obvious that in many instances, the first discovery is not an occurrence that can be known; the individual who made the discovery might not ever share his or her discoveries.
- **Disclosure**: When the discoverer of the vulnerability shares the specifics of the issue with the vendor or a disclosure institution, the vulnerability is said to have been disclosed. It is possible that the disclosure will be sent to a mailing list dedicated to vulnerabilities, such Bugtraq. Bugtraq is a mailing list with full disclosure that is moderated, and its purpose is to provide a venue for the in-depth debate and revelation of computer security flaws, including what these vulnerabilities are, how they may be exploited, and how they can be fixed. There is also the possibility

that the vendor or developer of the product will hear the news about the vulnerability directly.

- **Patch**: The date on which the first repair for the vulnerability is issued is known as the patch date. When a software vendor or developer makes available a software patch or configuration adjustment that fixes the vulnerability's fundamental defect, the vulnerability is considered to be correctable.
- **Public**: The date that the existence of the vulnerability was made publicly known is referred to as the "public date." This may occur when a patch is made available or when an announcement is made on a public forum. The public release date and the patch release date are frequently the same. A vulnerability might become known to the public in a few different ways. Either a story that appears in the media or a report that is issued by an incident response center might provide more information about the vulnerability. Once the disclosure gets out of hand, the most important thing is that the vulnerability becomes widely known to a huge number of people.
- **Scripting**: The date on which the first successful exploitation for the vulnerability is made public is referred to as the scripting date. An example of an exploit that is carried out automatically is a worm. Another illustration of this would be a piece of software that takes advantage of the flaw in order to grant its user administrative privileges on a distant computer.

It is important to note that the events in chronological order stated may appear in different sequences. For example, a vulnerability that is discovered by a malicious detector can be made public or a vulnerability may be discovered prior to a product release date: i.e. during the testing stage. The scripting date is also known as *exploit date*: It is the date on which first exploit for a vulnerability is available. An exploit is further classified into three kinds based on the time it was released. A positive day exploit is a type of exploit when an exploit is reported after the vulnerability is disclosed; it may appear before and after the patch date. A zero-day exploit occurs at the same time when a vulnerability is discovered. And a negative day exploit is a type of exploit when an exploit is reported before the discovery date of a vulnerability.

In practice, it is not possible to know all of the above dates for each vulnerability. Majority of vulnerability databases instead record the date on which the vulnerability-related information is available in the public platform. Ideally, the disclosure date or the public date is attributed as the discovery date.

Moreover, a vulnerability status is related to the events occurred in accordance to the lifecycle. The vulnerability based on its status can be defined as:

- **Unknown vulnerability:** These are the vulnerabilities that are present in the software but are not yet discovered.
- **Disclosed vulnerability:** These are the vulnerabilities that are discovered and are notified to a disclosure institution or the vendor.
- **Public vulnerability:** These are the vulnerabilities that are made public either by a vendor advisory, patch, or by other means.
- **Exploited vulnerability:** These are the vulnerabilities that are either exploited or there exists an automated exploit.

Let us take an example that considers the several stages of a single vulnerability's lifecycle and its current position. Ova Software Co., a provider of software, is working on the SecureAIProduct project. A programmer working for Ova Software Co. creates a code for SecureAIProduct 2023 that has a Cross-Site Scripting (XSS) vulnerability. When the programmer uploads the code to a CVS repository, the vulnerability is already there at that time. The date that SecureAI OS was initially made available to the public is the same day that the vulnerability was made public. The vulnerability will not be documented until it is uncovered by a detector, Mihika. It is a secret up to the point that Mihika reveals it to CERT/CC or to the vendor. In the end, Ova Software Co. will provide a fix, and on the same day Mihika will inform Bugtraq about the vulnerability, she will also post a note about it. Therefore, the date in question serves as both the patch date and the public disclosure date for the vulnerability. After some time, an automated exploit is made public, at which point the vulnerability is said to be scripted.

2.1.5 Vulnerability types

The vulnerabilities that are present in a piece of software can be arranged into groups according to the underlying behavior of the flaws or the many ways in which they might be exploited by an attacker. Before copying the material into the buffer, for instance, the developer may always do a check for the LENGTH variable first. Memory that is only temporarily used for storing information is referred to as a buffer. If more data than the buffer's defined size is allocated to the buffer, then the buffer will overflow, which will cause the additional data to outflow into other buffers. This will happen if the buffer is assigned more data than its defined size. Malicious users will utilize the additional data to store particular instructions that might be used to run malicious programs and get access to the system. They will do this by using the extra data. When a developer makes this kind of error when writing, it might lead to a vulnerability known as a buffer overflow vulnerability.

In this regard, there exist many different types of instances that may result in vulnerability. The National Vulnerability Database (NVD) repository recognized 13 types of vulnerabilities that may occur in a software system. A brief description of the types of vulnerabilities is given in the following:

- **Denial of service (DoS)**: It is considered a cyberattack when an adversary takes action that renders a computer or network resource temporarily or permanently inaccessible to the targeted computer system.
- **Code execution**: It takes place when a malicious user exploits a vulnerability in the system in order to execute any command remotely. The malicious software might be installed by the attacker, who could then remotely exploit the vulnerability that is present on the system that is being targeted.
- **Buffer overflow**: When a computer programmer allocates memory in an erroneous manner and then fails to release an allocated block of memory that is no longer required, a memory leak of this type is called buffer overflow.
- **Memory corruption**: A vulnerability can be said to exist when the contents of a memory location are accidentally altered without an explicit assignment being made to that place.
- **Structured query language (SQL) injection**: It is a term that refers to an injection method, which is utilized by an adversary in order to execute harmful SQL statements that are placed in the database server of an application.
- **Cross-site scripting (XSS)**: It is a form of injection attack in which a malicious script can be executed within a legitimate website or online application by an attacker.
- **Directory traversal**: It is a vulnerability in the hypertext transfer protocol (HTTP) that allows attackers to access files and directories and run commands outside of the folder that contains the web root.
- **HTTP response splitting**: It is a type of vulnerability that enables an attacker to construct an output stream by inputting a single HTTP

request to a web server, and the output stream is inferred as two replies rather than one.

- **Bypass something**: A vulnerability of this type enables a bypass of the authentication process, which can subsequently be used for nefarious purposes.
- **Gain information**: This vulnerability allows a local or remote adversary to obtain privileges in the affected application via a malicious program.
- **Gain privilege**: It is a form of vulnerability that provides the attacker with heightened access to the network as well as the data and applications that are linked with it.
- **Cross-site request forgery**: It is a form of attack that encourages users of a web application in which they are currently authenticated to carry out actions that they do not want to.
- **File inclusion**: It is a kind of vulnerability that enables an attacker to access unauthorized or sensitive files that are available on the web server or to execute malicious files on the web server. Additionally, an attacker can execute files on the web server.

During the process of vulnerability discovery, one of the most important things to keep in mind is the possibility that a vulnerability revealed of a certain kind may be influenced by the discovery of vulnerabilities of other types. In the same way that it may be ascribed to the occurrence of code execution type vulnerabilities, it could be attributable to the occurrence of buffer overflow type vulnerabilities. This may mean that the process of discovering vulnerabilities is a dependent process; that is, the discovery of one vulnerability may in some manner induce the discovery of another vulnerability.

The NVD data used by CVEDetails provides an easy way to use the vulnerability-related information for all software. The CVEDetails provides a tabular view of vulnerabilities categorized by their types. Table 2.1 provides the tabular view of vulnerabilities accounted from year 1999 to 2023 in each type. It can be noticed that a total of 23.1% of vulnerabilities are of code execution kind followed by 14.9% of denial of service type. Figure 2.2 presents a bar graph related to the number of vulnerabilities by their type. It has been noticed that software belonging to the class operating system may only account for a select few types of vulnerabilities when compared to software belonging to the class browser. As a result, the pattern of behavior of the vulnerability finding phenomena may follow differently across various software classes. This is due to the fact that some sorts of vulnerabilities that

Table 2.1 Number of vulnerabilities by their types (CveDetails, 2019).

Year	# of Vulnerabilities	File inclusion	CSRF	Gain Privileges	Gain Information	Bypass something	HTTP response splitting	Directory traversal	XSS	SQL injection	Memory corruption	Overflow	Code execution	DoS
1999	894			103	16	25		7	2			172	112	177
2000	1020			139	19	48		20	4	2	1	206	208	257
2001	1677	2		220	36	83		124	34	7		297	403	403
2002	2156	14	2	199	76	127		103	200	41	2	435	553	498
2003	1527	16		144	69	62	1	60	129	50	2	372	477	381
2004	2451	38	5	134	96	145	12	111	291	148	3	408	614	580
2005	4935	100	11	221	261	289	15	202	786	604	21	657	1627	838
2006	6610	849	18	184	272	267	8	322	1302	967	91	666	2719	893
2007	6520	700	69	242	326	267	14	338	883	706	95	954	2601	1101
2008	5632	170	83	188	268	288	7	362	807	1101	128	699	2310	894
2009	5736	138	115	223	302	337	9	323	852	963	188	698	2185	1035
2010	4653	73	86	238	284	234	8	276	605	520	342	671	1714	1102
2011	4155	17	58	206	408	197	7	109	470	294	351	723	1334	1221
2012	5297	14	166	250	391	344	13	122	759	243	423	828	1459	1425
2013	5191	1	123	274	510	352	7	110	650	155	366	846	1186	1455
2014	7939	2	264	239	2107	457	12	204	1103	304	420	839	1572	1599
2015	6504	5	248	366	752	577	12	151	784	221	749	1081	1830	1793
2016	6454	7	86	601	866	444	15	99	498	94	717	1219	1496	2028
2017	14714	18	327	459	1638	629	11	278	1518	508	745	2465	3004	3157
2018	16557	31	461	247	1227	708	11	544	2048	517	400	2120	3041	1856
2019	17344	57	535	202	913	712	10	475	2391	552	488	1244	3201	1346
2020	18325	37	402	310	1198	966	14	415	2183	464	409	1528	3251	1352
2021	20171	46	506	261	777	879	5	531	2714	741	483	1660	3851	1838
2022	25227	54	744	216	680	1056	8	695	3407	1789	421	2235	4064	2058
2023	10442	23	298	217	195	473	3	263	1839	834	146	793	1821	850
Total	202,131	2412	4607	6083	13,687	9966	202	6244	26,259	11,825	6991	23,816	46,633	30,137

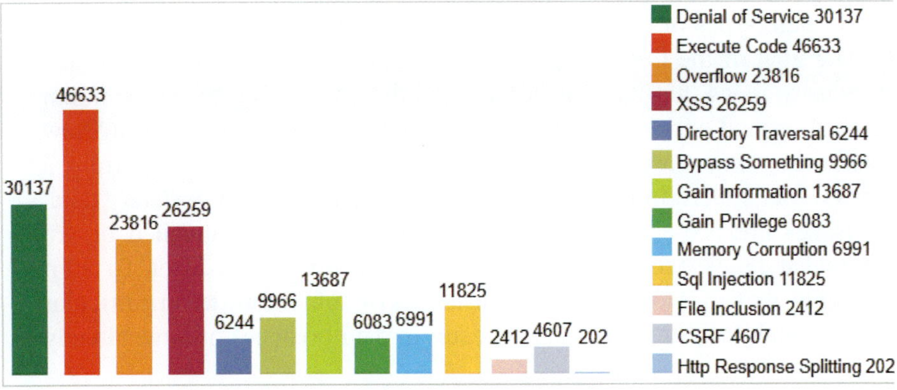

Figure 2.2 Vulnerabilities by their type (CveDetails, 2019).

are unique to operating systems have the potential to affect the identification of other types of vulnerabilities that may constitute a substantial danger owing to the fact that the operating system is responsible for memory management of the system and that it is possible for it to handle all software processes.

Any vulnerability that is present in the software might cause the production of further vulnerabilities, which is not the case for vulnerabilities that are related to software in the browser class. As a result, the process of finding vulnerabilities in software is significantly impacted by the types of vulnerabilities that are present in the software.

2.2 Software Vulnerability Standards

Disclosures of vulnerabilities often contain information for subjectively or quantitatively analyzing the severity of a vulnerability, which is done with the intention of assisting security managers. When trying to discover and categorize software vulnerabilities, it is vital to have knowledge of both the standards and the sources of security weaknesses. There are several different standards available, and any of these may be used to map a vulnerability. This section gives an overview of the many standards that may be used to identify a vulnerability based on different factors. These standards can be found further discussed in the following subsection.

2.2.1 Common vulnerabilities and exposures (CVE)

A public lexicon or catalogue of cybersecurity risks and events that are present in certain digital products is known as common vulnerabilities and exposures, or CVE for short. Vulnerabilities and exposures are two of the most prevalent types of cybersecurity occurrences that are catalogued by the CVE. The goal of the CVE Program is to discover, describe, and catalogue cybersecurity flaws that have been made public. According to the common vulnerabilities and exposures database, a vulnerability or exposure is a "flaw in a software, firmware, hardware, or service component resulting from a weakness" that cybercriminals can use to obtain sensitive or proprietary data. These issues are present in digital assets that have been launched or are operational and have been disclosed by the manufacturer of the asset. To put it more simply, these are already known instances of vulnerabilities in particular products, which have the potential to result in data breaches or have already done so.

CVE is helpful because it facilitates quick data correlation on a vulnerability across numerous information sources that are compatible with CVE. This makes it easier to track down potential exploits. For instance, if you possess a security tool that generates reports that contain references to CVE IDs, you will be able to access information about fixes that are stored in a different database that is compatible with CVE. CVE also gives you a starting point from which to evaluate the breadth of coverage provided by your tools. You will be able to assess which tools are most useful and suitable for the requirements of your organization by using the common IDs provided by CVE since you will know precisely what each tool protects against. Additionally, if the security advisories that your company receives include CVEs, you can check to see if your vulnerability scanners check for this threat, and then determine whether or not your intrusion detection system has the appropriate attack signatures to identify attempts to exploit particular vulnerabilities. This is possible if the security advisories include CVEs. If you construct or maintain systems for customers, the inclusion of CVEs in advisories will assist you in directly identifying any patches from the vendors of the commercial software products used in those systems (provided that the vendor fix site is compatible with CVE). This will be the case regardless of whether you develop or maintain the systems.

Each vulnerability or exposure that is discovered by a reporter is allocated a CVE ID. A CVE ID is the number portion of a CVE Record represented as CVE-YYYY-NNNNN. For example, a developer of software discovers a flaw in their program that weakens its security and makes it possible for unauthorized users to access confidential information. They communicate the information to the appropriate parties and acquire a unique CVE ID, such as "CVE-2023-12345." This vulnerability is listed on the CVE Record and may be used to track and refer to it in updates, security bulletins, and other information. The CVE entry includes a list of reference links to disclosures of the vulnerability, the date when the vulnerability was reported, and a link to the event in the National Vulnerability Database (NVD). The research, potential fixes, and frequent flaws that are connected with this vulnerability are also linked in this entry. This article establishes a linguistic standard that will be followed by other experts in the cybersecurity field and by internet technologies. If there is a need to make a reference to or discuss this event, CVE-2023-12345, the CVE entry offers a central location for information on the vulnerability. In addition, specialists in the field of cybersecurity might use the submission as a starting to begin the process of protecting this digital asset. Figure 2.3 provides a snippet of CVE Record that contains various details that are associated with a CVE ID.

The CVE Program was developed by the MITRE Corporation as a reaction to the absence of a systematic and universal method for recognizing and tracking cybersecurity vulnerabilities. It provides a comprehensive database of CVEs with the purpose of providing information on possible risks and informing organizations on how to safeguard their systems in a more effective manner. The database contains explanations of security holes, as well as IDs for vulnerabilities, impacted software versions, impact assessments, and instructions for fixing vulnerabilities. It enables organizations to monitor their exposures, determine the risk levels posed by them, and take preventative

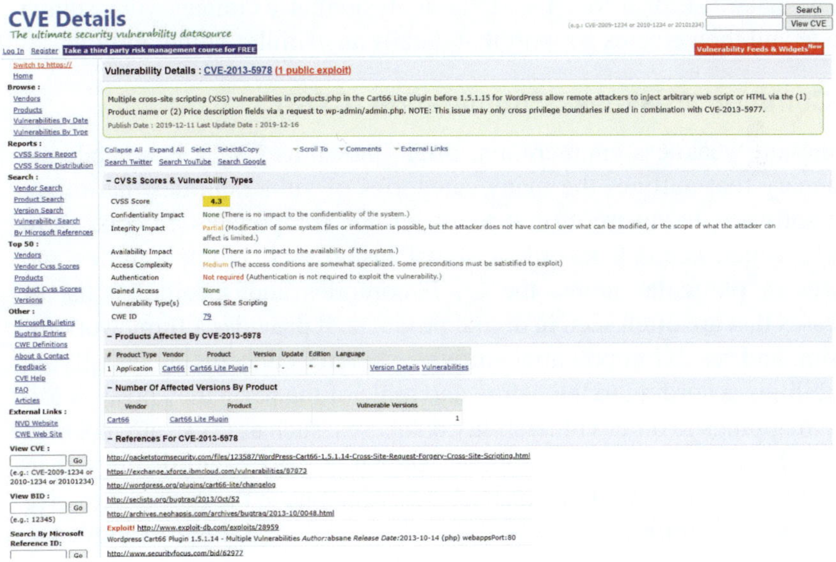

Figure 2.3 A snippet of CVE ID (Source: CVEDetails).

measures against them. MITRE has made it possible for organizations to have improved insight into the dangers posed by malicious actors while they are addressing security concerns as a result of the creation of such a system.

The CVE database can be used by developers and researchers in various ways such as:

- **Find flaws and fix them:** Developers may use the CVE List to check if the software they are working on has any known vulnerabilities and acquire information on how to fix them. For instance, you might use the CVE List to locate the security flaw in their program, and then utilize the information that is supplied to resolve the issue and implement an advancement for their application.
- **Prioritize vulnerabilities:** CVE allows developers to prioritize which vulnerabilities should be addressed first by classifying the kind of vulnerability and the possible effect of that issue. You may, for instance, use CVE to identify a vulnerability as "cross-site scripting." After that, you will be able to resolve this high-severity vulnerability in a timely manner. This vulnerability gives an intruder the opportunity to insert malicious code into a web page.
- **Integration with safety systems:** Integrating a piece of software with security tools that make use of CVE to automatically find and report vulnerabilities is something that developers can do. For instance, you may make use of a tool for static analysis that examines your source code and then creates a report that details any similar vulnerabilities.

2.2.2 Common Weakness Enumeration (CWE)

The common weakness enumeration, often known as CWE, is a catalogue or dictionary that outlines the many categories of vulnerabilities that might exist in software, hardware, firmware, or service components. In contrast to the CVE, which keeps a record of actual instances of vulnerabilities and exposures in particular items, the CWE compiles and specifies a list of weaknesses that are often seen in digital products. It provides a framework for discussing and resolving potential software security concerns by classifying vulnerabilities according to the nature and scale of the harm they pose. Additionally, mappings to other vulnerability databases, such as CVE, are included in the CWE. The actual vulnerabilities, known as CVEs, are distinguished from the underlying flaws, known as CWEs, which have the potential to give rise to such vulnerabilities. The CWE does not focus on a single example but rather gives definitions for several types of flaws that are common.

The purpose of the CWE, more so than that of the CVE, is to make available a standard language for the purpose of communicating about cybersecurity. In addition to this, it classifies weaknesses according to both their occurrence and kind, which helps characterize the shortcomings. When developing cybersecurity solutions, the CWE considers all of these minute nuances. Software developers and security workers are able to classify and have a better understanding of the many types of software faults when they make use of CWE. This enables them to prioritize the most important vulnerabilities and address them in a timely manner. In addition to this, it offers a consistent vocabulary for discussing and expressing software flaws, which helps to enhance communication and cooperation across various teams and organizations. For example, CWE-327, which is an example of a CWE entry, is headed "Use of a Broken or Risky Cryptographic Algorithm." Each item in the CWE defines a common flaw, including where it manifests, how frequently it does so, and how dangerous it is. It also describes the connections between the CW-327 weakness and other issues and offers CVE links to particular vulnerabilities that are brought about by the bug.

The Top 25 CWEs for 2022 are detailed in Table 2.2, along with their respective severity ratings.

The CWE could be used in various ways such as:

- When prioritizing which vulnerabilities to fix, developers may use CWE to categorize the kind of vulnerability and its possible effect. For instance, "CWE-79: Improper Neutralization of Input During Web Page Generation ('Cross-site Scripting')" describes a common type of vulnerability. This critical flaw, which allows an attacker to insert malicious code into a web page, may then be fixed.
- CWE allows developers to spot and repair the most prevalent forms of code flaws. If you use CWE to find a "CWE-835: Loop with Unreachable Exit Condition ('Infinite Loop')" in your code, you may fix it by adding an explicit exit condition to the loop.
- CWE is also useful since it provides a framework for ranking the severity of software flaws in a transparent, consistent, and open fashion. It is an open, community-driven project serving the interests of people in government, the academy, and business. It enables businesses to utilize the common weakness scoring system (CWSS), which ranks the severity of software code flaws, to address vulnerabilities in their existing apps and shape their future acquisitions.

Table 2.2 The CWE Top 25 (Mitre, 2022).

Rank	ID	Name	Score
1	CWE-787	Out-of-bounds Write	64.20
2	CWE-79	Improper Neutralization of Input During Web Page Generation ('Cross-site Scripting')	45.97
3	CWE-89	Improper Neutralization of Special Elements used in an SQL Command ('SQL Injection')	22.11
4	CWE-20	Improper Input Validation	20.63
5	CWE-125	Out-of-bounds Read	17.67
6	CWE-78	Improper Neutralization of Special Elements used in an OS Command ('OS Command Injection')	17.53
7	CWE-416	Use After Free	15.50
8	CWE-22	Improper Limitation of a Pathname to a Restricted Directory ('Path Traversal')	14.08
9	CWE-352	Cross-site Request Forgery (CSRF)	11.53
10	CWE-434	Unrestricted Upload of File with Dangerous Type	9.56
11	CWE-476	NULL Pointer Dereference	7.15
12	CWE-502	Deserialization of Untrusted Data	6.68
13	CWE-190	Integer Overflow or Wraparound	6.53
14	CWE-287	Improper Authentication	6.35
15	CWE-798	Use of Hard-coded Credentials	5.66
16	CWE-862	Missing Authorization	5.53
17	CWE-77	Improper Neutralization of Special Elements used in a Command ('Command Injection')	5.42
18	CWE-306	Missing Authentication for Critical Function	5.15
19	CWE-119	Improper Restriction of Operations within the Bounds of a Memory Buffer	4.85
20	CWE-276	Incorrect Default Permissions	4.84
21	CWE-918	Server-Side Request Forgery (SSRF)	4.27
22	CWE-362	Concurrent Execution using Shared Resource with Improper Synchronization ('Race Condition')	3.57
23	CWE-400	Uncontrolled Resource Consumption	3.56
24	CWE-611	Improper Restriction of XML External Entity Reference	3.38
25	CWE-94	Improper Control of Generation of Code ('Code Injection')	3.32

2.2.3 CVSS metric

To assist security administrators, vulnerability disclosures typically include information for assessing a vulnerability's severity qualitatively or quantitatively. It includes a CVSS metric and various parameters for each CVE disclosed. The common vulnerability scoring system (CVSS) is designed to measure the severity of a software by utilizing various characteristics that affect a vulnerability. It comprises some factors that produce a numeric base score rating from 0 to 10, which reflects a qualitative severity rating. The base score is computed in terms of impact (I) and exploitability (E) factors using the following equation:

$$\text{BaseScore} = \left(\frac{3I}{5} + \frac{2E}{5} - \frac{3}{2}\right) \times 1.176. \tag{2.1}$$

Moreover, the impact and exploitability scores are themselves calculated based on various sets of characteristics a vulnerability has had when it was discovered. The impact metric measures the significant consequences of an exploited vulnerability and the exploitability metric measures the conditions required to exploit a vulnerability. Critical vulnerabilities are considered to be the highest priority flaws. These signified exposures, if exploited, could lead to consequences that affect IT assets. These flaws should be addressed immediately owing to the significant threat on the software. It has been observed in CVSS guide that the critical vulnerabilities are marked with high and medium risk levels. The risk levels are set by vulnerability bulletin analysts, security product vendors, or application vendors and are dependent on various factors considering a vulnerability being successfully exploited. Several factors are evaluated when a given vulnerability is measured critical: an attacker's ability to remotely exploit a flaw, obtaining privileges after a successful attack, and the degree of loss of confidentiality, integrity, and availability (Mell et.al., 2007).

The base score provides an overview to severity rating of a vulnerability. A vulnerability can be assigned with any of the four different severities: critical, high, medium, and low. Table 2.3 provides the range of base scores along with the severity rating. As per the CVSS guide, a vulnerability whose score lies in the critical range can be used by the attackers to run arbitrary code and require no user authorization and have a high likelihood of exploitation. For these types of vulnerabilities, it is advised to provide a patch as soon as possible. A vulnerability having a high key impact may

Table 2.3 CVSS base score severity rating.

CVSS base score range	Severity rating
0.1–3.9	Low
4.0–6.9	Medium
7.0–8.9	High
9.0–10.0	Critical

gather sensitive data and requires partial user interaction for the exploitation. A medium severity level requires the attacker to manipulate individual victim via gaining respective privileges for successful exploitation. A low severity level vulnerability has a very little impact on an individual user and requires local or physical access in order to exploit a vulnerability.

References

Conte, 1986

Beizer, B. (2003). Software testing techniques. Dreamtech Press.

Pfleeger, C. P., & Pfleeger, S. S. (2007). *Security in Computing*. Upper Saddle River, NJ, USA: Prentice Hall.

Computer Science and Telecommunications Board. (2001). *Computers at Risk: Safe Computing In the Information Age* . Washington, DC, Computers: National Academy Press.

Krsul, I. V. (1998). *Software Vulnerability Analysis.* Retrieved from Purdue University: https://docs.lib.purdue.edu/dissertations/AAI9900214/

CERT, 2019

Arbaugh, W. A., Fithen, W. L., & McHugh, J. (2000). Windows of vulnerability: A case study analysis. Computer, 33(12), 52-59.

CveDetails. (2019). *Vulnerabilities By Type*. Retrieved from CveDetails: http s://www.cvedetails.com/vulnerabilities-by-types.php

Mitre, 2022

Mell, P., Scarfone, K., & Romanosky, S. (2007, June). *A Complete Guide to the Common Vulnerability Scoring System*. Retrieved from First.org: https: //www.first.org/cvss/v2/guide

3

Vulnerability Discovery Models (VDMs)

The phrase "vulnerability discovery models" refers to a collection of approaches that have been developed with the purpose of locating and exploiting security flaws in software systems. The process of developing these models has taken a long time and is still ongoing. It has been shaped by developments in computer technology as well as by shifting patterns in the threat landscape.

The development of automated software testing techniques occurred in the 1960s and 1970s, which coincided with the introduction of the first vulnerability finding models. These technologies were developed with the purpose of locating faults and mistakes in code within software systems. Due to the fact that these early models were not developed with the intention of discovering security flaws, they were only somewhat successful in doing so. The VDMs may prove to be a beneficial technique for predicting different vulnerability characteristics. However, they are seen as analogous to software reliability growth models (SRGMs) that were developed to predict the potential faults present in a software that might be detected during the software testing and debugging process. The SRGMs are used to address the issue of determining how reliable a piece of software is by counting the number of errors that it has produced. It describes the behavior of software failures in relation to the passage of time. As flaws in the program are found and corrected, it will become less likely to malfunction and will have a higher degree of reliability. As a result, the models are used during the testing phase to apply to both observed and past failures, and they are then analyzed using statistical inference.

The development of increasingly advanced software reliability models occurred in the 1980s and 1990s as a direct result of the advent of the internet and the ever-increasing significance of maintaining network security. These models were primarily concerned with locating and exploiting flaws in network protocols, application software, and operating systems. Instruments such as port scanners, network sniffers, and penetration testing frameworks were among the tools that were offered.

Both vulnerability databases and bug bounty programs made their debut in the early years of the new millennium. These projects offered researchers with incentives to uncover and report security flaws in software systems, which was a win-win situation. They also resulted in the creation of more comprehensive vulnerability finding models that integrated manual testing with automated technologies. These models were developed as a direct result of the vulnerability disclosures.

Over the course of the past several years, machine learning and artificial intelligence have seen an increased amount of application in vulnerability identification methods. These models make use of data-driven methodologies in order to detect possible vulnerabilities and rank them in order of priority for future research. In general, the development of vulnerability discovery models reflects the continual evolution of the software industry as a whole as well as the shifting nature of the dangers that it faces. It is expected that vulnerability identification methods will continue to develop over time in order to accommodate new problems and possibilities. This is because software systems are becoming increasingly complicated and linked.

3.1 Vulnerability Discovery Modeling: Introduction

Vulnerability discovery models are parametric functions based on time to describe the discovery phenomenon of software vulnerabilities pertaining to a single or multiple software release(s). They operate based on historical vulnerability data, which may contain various events occurring over the lifetime of a vulnerability, such as the date on which the vulnerability was discovered or the date on which it was disclosed. The VDMs utilize the CVE information to mathematically predict the vulnerabilities to be discovered over the time. The models may be utilized to characterize a variety of characteristics, including the overall number of vulnerabilities that are present in a software, the pace at which vulnerabilities are discovered, and other similar characteristics.

VDMs are helpful mathematical functions that may be applied in order to gain an understanding of the behavior of vulnerabilities that are accounted for in a software system. Various software systems, such as operating systems, browsers, application software, and so on, each follow their own unique pattern when it comes to the detection of vulnerabilities. Therefore, a

VDM may be appropriately applied to a certain software system in order to investigate the vulnerability characteristics it possesses. In order to demonstrate the usefulness of a VDM, we will use the example of a software SecureAIProduct by Ova Software Co.

After the SecureAIProduct is made available to the public, the following average number of vulnerabilities are found each month as follows: 6, 3, 4, 7, 8, 12, 8, 6, 3, 2, 1, 1. The vulnerability data may be represented as an S-shaped curve, and a VDM that uses a logistic growth pattern might be able to appropriately anticipate the vulnerability data. It is possible to further extend the curve so that it can capture the behavior of vulnerabilities over the following half year. It is possible that the Ova Software Co. will make use of this information in order to schedule vendor detectors and the appropriate resources needed to fix the potential future vulnerabilities.

However, even our straightforward example illustrates some of the difficulties that come with modeling vulnerability discovery. Is Ova Software Co. simply addressing one issue at a time with each patch, or do their patches address many vulnerabilities at once? What exactly is a risk factor? If a piece of source code has a buffer overflow in two similar methods that are quite close to one another, would this count as one vulnerability or two? According to the definition of vulnerabilities that we presented in Section 2.2.1, there are two distinct instances of a vulnerability if there are two instances of a buffer overflow. Estimating and forecasting the vulnerability characteristics of software may be made easier with the use of vulnerability discovery models, which may prove to be a beneficial tool. A standardized nomenclature is necessary before we can have an intelligent conversation on VDMs.

3.2 Preliminary Concepts of Vulnerability Discovery Modeling

VDMs have the potential to be a useful approach for anticipating various vulnerability features. On the other hand, they are considered to be comparable to software reliability growth models (SRGMs), which are the mathematical models that were built to forecast the possible faults that may be present in a software and that may be discovered throughout the process of software testing and debugging. According to Lyu's research from 1996, "A software reliability model specifies the general form of the software failure process as a function of factors such as fault introduction, fault removal, and the operational environment" (Lyu, 1996). The SRGMs are used for the problem of determining how reliable a piece of software is by counting the number of errors that it has produced. It describes the behavior of software failures in relation to the passage of time. As faults in the program are found and corrected, it will become less likely to malfunction and will have a higher degree of reliability. As a result, the models are used during the testing phase to apply to both observed and past failures, and they are then analyzed using statistical inference.

In this part, we will go through the basic ideas behind software vulnerability discovery models as well as other metrics linked with VDMs. First, we will give a brief overview of the differences between VDMs and SRGMs. In addition, we discuss the assumptions that the VDMs are built upon and the advantages that those assumptions provide to the software development process. We start with some standard distribution functions and then derive the vulnerability-finding phenomena from those functions. In the next sections, we carry out a full discussion on non-homogeneous Poisson process (NHPP) based vulnerability modeling in order to give the readers an understanding of the fundamental principles behind NHPP-based vulnerability finding models.

3.2.1 Comparison of SRGMs and VDMs

The dependability of a program is assumed to be proportional to the number of flaws it possesses, which is the fundamental premise around which SRMs are founded. As faulty components are located and eliminated, the system will have fewer failures and will, as a result, be more reliable. Therefore, software reliability models (SRMs) anticipate the product's reliability by applying statistical approaches to the failures that were seen during software testing and operation.

These models may be used to make estimates about certain characteristics of the system, such as the number of faults that are still present in the system and the times at which those faults could produce failures. These estimations can be used as a basis for determining the extent of further testing that will be necessary to satisfy reliability criteria.

Along the same lines, the VDMs are constructed using the same fundamentals as the SRGMs. On the other hand, the purpose of a VDM is not to identify a susceptible module but rather to quantify the faults that are already present in software and that have the potential to result in vulnerabilities. Despite the fact that SRGMs have been utilized for the majority of the previous several decades, the process of assessing the security of software has only just begun to quantify the vulnerabilities. Numerous investigations have shown that the VDMs are regarded to be a specialization of the SRGMs. In spite of this, actual research has shown that security flaws are not the same as regular bugs in a number of important respects (Massacci & Nguyen, 2014). Roger Needham contended that there is a sociological explanation behind this discrepancy. Needham's argument was based on the fact that there is a community of people who make it their personal priority to make the wrong things happen, typically in other people's computers (Needham, 2002).

It is essential for the readers to understand both the definition of the VDMs and the methodology behind their application in the estimation of the vulnerabilities. It was Omar Alhazmi and Yashwant Malaiya who demonstrated the usefulness of SRGMs for software vulnerabilities and coined the term "vulnerability discovery models" (Alhazmi & Malaiya, 2005a). In contrast to the software dependability sector, the security sector does not have a universally accepted terminology. Nonetheless, Gopalakrishna *et al.* (2015) consider the phrase "vulnerability likelihood" when describing the safety of a system; however, their definition incorporated probabilistic methodologies in contrast to VDMs (Gopalakrishna & Spafford, 2005).

In this section, as well as the rest of the book, we are going to make use of the term "vulnerability discovery model" since it appears to have garnered the greatest attention from readers. On the other hand, it does not seem to have been properly defined as of yet; the definition that we prefer and that we shall use here was proposed by Andy Ozmant as:

> A vulnerability discovery model, also known as a VDM, is a model that explains the general form of the reliance of the vulnerability discovery process on the primary elements that impact it, such as the introduction of vulnerabilities, the removal of vulnerabilities, the amount of effort put into detectors, and the operating environment. (Ozment, 2007)

The term VDM is used to refer to models that have been applied to vulnerability findings, whereas the term SRGM refers to models that have been applied to software failures. However, it is crucial to highlight that the same model may be used both as an SRM and a VDM. The majority of the work that has been done so far takes previously developed SRGMs and applies them to the problem of developing VDMs. The VDMs primarily provide two advantageous characteristics. First, the possible amount of vulnerabilities in a software system, as well as the rate at which new vulnerabilities are discovered. In addition, it provides the mean time to next vulnerability (MTTNV) is found in a software. In the field of software reliability engineering, the notion of mean time between failure (MTBF) is synonymous with the term mean time to next vulnerability (MTTNV).

3.2.2 VDM assumptions

Since VDMs and SRGMs behave similarly, researchers have assumed that the same assumptions that apply to SRGMs also apply to VDMs. However, not all of the assumptions that were taken into consideration for SRGMs are appropriate when applied to VDMs. Andy Ozment supported the same viewpoint and claimed that the obstacles that VDMs often encounter include time, environment, independence, and static code (Ozment, 2007). These standards must be followed since they are the basis for the VDMs' accuracy and efficacy.

The efficiency of the VDMs' prediction skills is reflected in the data to which they are applied, and the VDMs themselves reflect that effectiveness. As is the case with SRGMs, it is recommended that calendar time and execution time data be used in accordance with the model that is being studied. Calendar time, often known as fault count data, is utilized by the majority of SRGMs. The same is true for vulnerability data management systems (VDMs), despite the fact that gathering accurate chronological data on vulnerability discovery is a challenging issue. This is because the process of discovering vulnerabilities is impacted both by internal and external reporters. It might be challenging to get an accurate measurement of the efforts that an external reporter puts in, such as their count and their expertise. In VDMs, the process of counting the number of instances of vulnerabilities found in software systems requires standardizing the calendar time. In addition, the amount of work that must be put in to find a vulnerability depends on a variety of factors, including the number of people who report it, the amount of time they spend doing it, and their level of expertise.

In addition to this, it is essential to properly manage the operating system in which the programmed will be used. Therefore, in order to successfully replicate the process of discovery, the VDMs are utilized, and the same environment that they were developed upon is supplied to them. In the event that either the operating environment or the method of detection are altered, the model will be unable to produce correct results. It is thought that the vulnerabilities are found by themselves. However, many studies have supported the idea that vulnerability data is dependent. This is because vulnerability detectors that are malicious always search for other instances of the vulnerability (of the same type) that has been discovered recently, and it is possible for a developer to make the same mistake more than once (Gopalakrishna & Spafford, 2005). Because the vast bulk of the code is shared with other modules, this might result in the identification of other security flaws. In light of this, it is imperative that this assumption be taken into consideration before applying VDMs to the vulnerability data, since doing so might lead to the discovery of many occurrences of the same vulnerability. In many instances, vulnerabilities that are reliant on one another are coupled with one another and treated as a single occurrence.

It has been seen that several kinds of calendar time software reliability models based on the non-homogeneous Poisson process (NHPP) have been developed in the literature to describe the stochastic behavior of the number of defects identified when the process is being debugged. This is something that has been observed. The release of a piece of software is always accompanied by a substantial number of bugs, both known and unknown. Testing carried out during the operating phase often has as its primary objective the identification of any software flaws or vulnerabilities that may exist. A vulnerability is a subset of a flaw that may have been identified by a software vendor or a reporter, and each vulnerability in the program has an equal chance of being exploited by either malicious or benign users. The complexity and scale of the software program means that vulnerabilities might develop in a big number, and the chance of detecting vulnerabilities in a short amount of time is quite low. This is because of the complexity and size of the software program. As a result of the law of rare event, the process of finding vulnerabilities may be modeled using the Poisson process.

3.2.3 Distribution functions to depict the software vulnerability process

The previous discussion on the vulnerability discovery process enables us to define it in terms of their discovery pattern. Thus, the vulnerabilities that are discovered in a software system are all due to the efforts that a reporter makes while searching for any mistakes that could lead to any exposure. This behavior is used to establish a link between how the vulnerabilities could be discovered or disclosed in a software system. The phenomenon could be depicted using various distribution functions that are available in the literature and provide an accurate estimation of the vulnerabilities in a software system.

Here, we provide some important distribution functions and their linkage to the vulnerability discovery phenomenon.

3.2.3.1 Exponential distribution

The exponential distribution is one of the distributions that is utilized rather frequently in predicting the expected number of flaws or vulnerabilities due to the fact that it has a constant rate. It is an indication that the process of discovering vulnerabilities is equally distributed and that each vulnerability has the same likelihood of being identified during the process of discovering vulnerabilities. It is anticipated that the finding of software vulnerabilities would follow an exponential distribution in the majority of the software testing efforts. As a result, it is not unreasonable to take into consideration exponential distribution for the process of vulnerability discovery.

The fact that this distribution has a constant instantaneous failure rate, which helps to decrease the complexity of the mathematics required in analysis, is the primary reason for the numerous uses of this distribution in the field of reliability studies. However, the constant failure rate has the limitation that it can only be used when the discovery of vulnerability any moment throughout its operation is equal to its stage at the beginning of its activity. This is the only circumstance in which it is suitable to use the constant instantaneous failure rate. This is not the case in the majority of situations. As a result, the distribution is best adapted to modeling the vulnerability discovery that can be characterized by a constant failure rate but not for the overall life period. The memory-less property is a feature of exponential distribution that can be identified by its name. First, we will write the *PDF* of the distribution before moving on to the formal derivation of this characteristic.

$$f(t) = \frac{1}{\theta}\, e^{-\frac{t}{\theta}} = \lambda e^{-\lambda t}; \quad t \geq 0, \tag{3.1}$$

where λ is the rate parameter and can be considered as vulnerability discovery rate.

The cumulative density function, *CDF*, is given by

$$F(t) = (1 - e^{-rt}). \tag{3.2}$$

3.2.3.2 Weibull distribution

Within the field of reliability engineering, the Weibull distribution is among the distributions that are utilized the most frequently. Depending on the value of the shape parameter, β, this distribution may take on the properties of a variety of different distributions, making it a flexible and adaptable form of distribution. As was said before, exponential distribution has the disadvantage of having a danger function that is constant over the life of the component, despite the fact that it is utilized more frequently in reliability modeling. On the other hand, the exponential distribution might be considered a generalization of the Weibull distribution due to the adaptable character of the Weibull distribution.

In the vast majority of instances that occur in real life, the degree of vulnerability intensity increases at first but subsequently improves over the course of time. In order to account for this occurrence, the Weibull distribution has been shown to be effective while adopting this behavior of growing and reducing vulnerability intensity due to the value of its shape parameter. This behavior has been shown to be successful in capturing this phenomenon using Weibull distribution.

A function with three, two, or even just one parameter can be used to derive the Weibull probability density. The Weibull PDF with three parameters may be written as

$$f(t) = \frac{\beta}{\theta}\left(\frac{t-\gamma}{\theta}\right)^{\beta-1} e^{-\left(\frac{t-\gamma}{\theta}\right)^{\beta}}, \tag{3.3}$$

where $t,\ f(t) \geq 0$ or $\gamma, \beta,\ \theta > 0,\ -\infty < \gamma < \infty$ and θ is the scale parameter, β is the shape parameter (slope), and γ is the location parameter.

Setting $\gamma = 0$ allows one to derive the two-parameter Weibull PDF, which can then be written as

$$f(t) = \frac{\beta}{\theta}\left(\frac{t}{\theta}\right)^{\beta-1} e^{-\left(\frac{t}{\theta}\right)^{\beta}}. \tag{3.4}$$

And the Weibull PDF with a single parameter may be generated by setting $\gamma = 0$ and assuming $\beta = C$, where *C* is a constant or an assumed value.

$$f(t) = \frac{C}{\theta}\left(\frac{t}{\theta}\right)^{C-1} e^{-\left(\frac{t}{\theta}\right)^{C}}, \tag{3.5}$$

where the only variable that is not known is the scale parameter, denoted by θ. When formulating the one-parameter Weibull distribution, we keep in mind that the shape parameter β is already known through earlier research or experience with items with the same or comparable characteristics. One of the benefits of taking this approach is that it enables the analysis of datasets that include few or no discovered vulnerability in a time point.

If $F(t)$ can be taken as Weibull distribution function to examine the vulnerability discovery process, then:

$$F\left(t\right)=1-e^{-\left(\frac{t-\gamma}{\theta}\right)^{\beta}}. \tag{3.6}$$

In addition, it is clear that the instantaneous vulnerability detection rate can assume a variety of appearances depending on the value of β that is used, which is defined as follows:

$$\begin{array}{ll} \beta<0 & \text{decreasing} \\ \beta>0 & \text{increasing} \\ \beta=0 & \text{constant} \end{array}. \tag{3.7}$$

The Weibull distribution may be used to simulate many different aspects of life, depending on the values that are assigned to the parameters in the model.

3.2.3.3 Logistic distribution

In probability theory, the logistic distribution is a continuous distribution with a cumulative distribution function that looks like a logistic curve. The logistic distribution, along with the S-shaped pattern that comes from applying it, has seen widespread application across a wide variety of domains. It has widespread application in the field of reliability modeling, particularly in the area of software reliability. In logistic regression and feed forward neural networks, the distribution appears rather frequently. In terms of form, it is comparable to a normal distribution, but it has longer tailed and a larger kurtosis.

Real-world observations have shown that as detectors learn more about the software, the rate at which vulnerabilities are discovered in the early stages is lower than expected. This has been the case since the beginning of time. After gaining familiarity with the software, the detector could be able to readily uncover flaws in an exponential form, which would lead to the vulnerability discovery rate having an S-shaped character. Logistic distribution has the potential to reflect this quality of the vulnerability detection process, which is necessary for the assertion of this perspective.

The logistic distribution with two parameters can be written as

$$f\left(t\right)=\frac{b\left(1+\beta\right)e^{-bt}}{\left(1+\beta e^{-bt}\right)^{2}};t\geq 0,\ 0\leq b<1,\ \beta\geq 0. \tag{3.8}$$

The cumulative density function is given as

$$F(t) = \int_0^t f(s)\,ds = \frac{1 - e^{-bt}}{1 + \beta e^{-bt}}. \tag{3.9}$$

There is a further subtype of the logistic distribution that can be specified, and it is called the half logistic distribution. It is a one-parameter continuous probability distribution, and the PDF formula looks like this:

$$f(t) = \frac{2be^{-2bt}}{(1 + e^{-bt})^2}; t \geq 0,\ 0 \leq b \leq 1, \tag{3.10}$$

and the CDF is given as

$$F(t) = \int_0^t f(s)\,ds = \frac{1 - e^{-bt}}{1 + e^{-bt}}. \tag{3.11}$$

3.2.3.4 Gamma distribution

For modeling continuously positive and skewed variables, engineers, scientists, and businesspeople frequently turn to the Gamma distribution. One type of continuous probability distribution is known as the gamma distribution. This distribution has two parameters. In the case of the gamma distribution, the probability density function is

$$f(t) = \frac{1}{\Gamma(\alpha)\beta}\left(\frac{t}{\beta}\right)^{\alpha-1} e^{-\left(\frac{t}{\beta}\right)}; t \geq 0,\ \ \alpha, \beta > 0, \tag{3.12}$$

where α and β refer to the parameters for the shape and scale, respectively. The impact that the scale parameter β has on the Gamma distribution is to either expand or compress the range of the distribution. The term "standard Gamma distribution" refers to a Gamma distribution in which β is set equal to 1. If β is an integer, then the distribution is the total of β independent random variables that are exponentially distributed and each of which has a mean of α (which is equal to a rate parameter of α^{-1}), and if β is not an integer, then the distribution does not reflect the sum of any random variables. Gamma distribution is exponentially shaped and asymptotic to both the vertical and horizontal axes when $\alpha < 1$. When $\alpha = 1$ and scale parameter β, gamma distribution is the same as an exponential distribution of scale parameter (or mean) β. While α governs the shape of the distribution, when $\alpha < 1$, gamma distribution is exponentially shaped and asymptotic to both the vertical and horizontal axes. If $\alpha > 1$, then the Gamma distribution takes on the structure of a unimodal distribution that is skewed. As α increases in value, the skewness of the distribution becomes less extreme.

3.2.4 NHPP-based vulnerability discovery models

As was discussed before, VDMs are a unique kind of SRGMs that have their own set of characteristics. The sole distinction is that VDMs are applied to the vulnerability reporting or discovery data rather than the software fault data. It has been seen that a variety of calendar time software reliability models based on the non-homogeneous Poisson process (NHPP) have developed in the literature to describe the stochastic behavior of the number of defects identified when the process is being debugged. Readers of this book who are interested in gaining a more in-depth understanding of typical SRMs and the functional shapes they take might look into other publications that have been produced on the topic of software testing and reliability.

In the field of reliability engineering, the term "Poisson process" is the one that is most commonly used to describe a counting process. In the process of analyzing the dependability of hardware, NHPP has been utilized effectively to explain both improving and deteriorating patterns in reliability. In order to keep up with the latest developments in hardware reliability analysis, a large number of researchers suggested and verified many NHPP-based SRGM. During the testing and operational phases of software development, SRGM describes the failure occurrence and/or failure removal phenomena with regard to time (CPU time, calendar time, or execution time of test cases as unit of time) and/or resources spent on testing and debugging. On the similar lines, researchers have also treated the vulnerability discovery process to follow the exact skeleton of SRGMs. Models of the real system and its functioning have been developed using stochastic modeling for quite some time. Continuous and discrete stochastic processes are the two primary varieties of this sort of process. Counting process is one of the classes of discrete processes, and it is extensively used in the field of reliability engineering to represent the occurrence of a time-based event (such as failure, repair, etc.).

If a non-negative, integer-valued stochastic process, $N(t)$, reflects the total number of occurrences of an event in the range of time $[0, t]$, and if $N(t)$ meets the two conditions listed below, then we refer to that process as a counting process.

- If $t_1 < t_2$, then $N(t_1) \leq N(t_2)$.
- If $t_1 < t_2$, then $N(t_2) - N(t_1)$ is the number of occurrences of the event in the time interval $[t_1, t_2]$.

Take, as an illustration, the occurrence $N(t)$ of the purchase of cinema tickets. $N(t)$ is a counting process if the number of tickets bought up to the time t_1 is denoted by $N(t_1)$, and the number of tickets booked between the times t_1 and t_2 is denoted by $N(t_2) - N(t_1)$, with the stipulation that $N(t_1) \leq N(t_2)$. When a ticket is booked, then an event occurs.

Accordingly, the failure phenomenon described during the software testing process is modeled by the NHPP, and consequently, the vulnerability discovery phenomenon can be described using the counting process $\{N(t), t > 0\}$ and can be given as

$$\Pr\{N(t) = k\} = \frac{\Omega(t)^k e^{-\Omega(t)}}{k!}, \quad k = 0, 1, 2, \ldots. \tag{3.13}$$

That is, $N(t)$ has a Poisson distribution with expected value $E[N(t)] = \Omega(t)$ for $t > 0$. The vulnerability discovery function or the mean value function, $\Omega(t)$, represents the cumulative number of vulnerabilities discovered by time t and is the basic building block of all the NHPP models that exist in the literature.

3.2.5 VDM classification and literature

The present research on VDMs may be broken down into two primary categories: those that focus on time and those that emphasize effort. The time-based models take into consideration the discovery of vulnerabilities over the course of time, whereas the latter model quantifies the vulnerabilities depending on the amount of work that was put into their discovery.

3.2.5.1 Rescorla exponential model

Eric Rescorla made the initial suggestion for a VDM in the year 2005. Rescorla concluded that the vulnerabilities are being identified at an exponential rate but at a consistent rate. The Poisson process features were utilized by Rescorla in order to account for the amount of vulnerabilities found in a software per unit of time. According to Rescorla, (2005), the model assumed that the number of vulnerabilities revealed at any given time point or the vulnerability intensity is proportionate to the total number of vulnerabilities that are still to be detected. One possible mathematical model for the differential equation that illustrates the discovery situation is as follows:

$$\frac{d\Omega(t)}{dt} \propto (N - \Omega(t)). \tag{3.14}$$

The method of discovering vulnerabilities will, at a predetermined rate *r*, identify any remaining flaws that have not yet been found. The differential equation that was presented in eqn (3.12) may also be represented as

$$\frac{d\Omega(t)}{dt} = r\,(N - \Omega(t))\,. \tag{3.15}$$

The solution of eqn (3.15) can be found using the initial condition, $\Omega\,(0) = 0$. A closed form of eqn (3.16) can be written as

$$\Omega\,(t) = N\left(1 - e^{-rt}\right). \tag{3.16}$$

3.2.5.2 Alhazmi and Malaiya logistic (AML) model

In 2005, Alhazmi and Malaiya came up with the idea that would later become known as the AML model. The model assumed that the discovery pattern would evolve into an S-shaped (logistic) pattern over the course of some amount of time. Both Alhazmi and Malaiya argued in favor of the idea that the vulnerability discovery phenomena take place in three phases, which are known as the learning, linear, and saturation stages, respectively. Figure 3.1 illustrates the finding of the vulnerability occurring at various phases during the process.

The initial half of the illustration shows a level part of the curve. In this case, following the introduction of a software, the detectors require time to learn about the software; as a consequence, there were fewer reports of vulnerabilities. The detectors have started to get an understanding of the

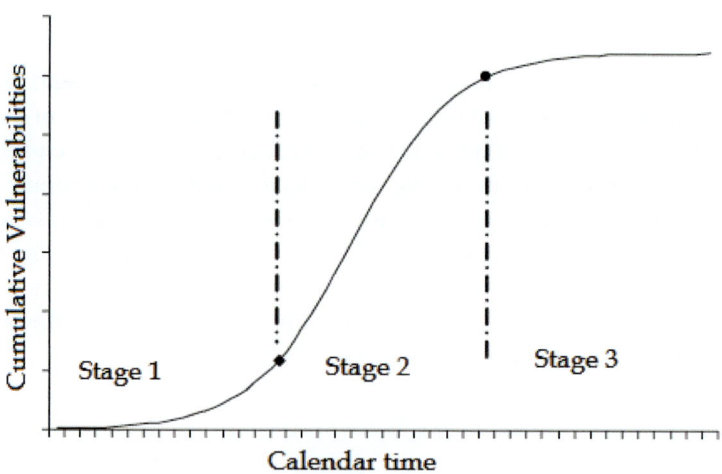

Figure 3.1 The three stages of the vulnerability discovery process (Source: Alhazmi & Malaiya 2005).

software and have started to collect sufficient information linked to any potential gaps that may exist in the software. The next segment of the curve, which is steeper, can be used to describe this stage. Detectors are now familiar with the software, and they understand how the software works; as a result, there has been an increase in the number of vulnerabilities that have been reported by the detector. In addition, the vast majority of users have consented to use the software, and its level of popularity has reached an all-time high. At this time, vulnerability detectors are likely to receive the greatest rewards. After that point, the discovery process reaches a plateau, which is represented by the segment of the curve that is flat. The majority of users have upgraded to a more recent version of the software, which has resulted in a fall in the discovery rate as well as a reduction in the number of vulnerability detection instances.

The differential equation proposed by Alhazmi and Malaiya to depict the behavior of vulnerability discovery process can be written as

$$\frac{d\Omega(t)}{dt} = r\Omega\left(t\right)\left(N - \Omega\left(t\right)\right). \tag{3.17}$$

The solution of eqn (3.17) can be given as

$$\Omega\left(t\right) = \frac{N}{1 + NCe^{-rNt}}, \tag{3.18}$$

where N, r, and C are the parameters of the model representing total number of vulnerabilities, vulnerability discovery rate, and constant introduced while solving eqn (3.18), respectively.

The suggested model was evaluated by Alhazmi and Malaiya by fitting the model to a variety of software encompassing a wide range of software classes. The software included browsers, Linux and Windows operating systems, and more. The majority of the datasets had chi-square goodness of fit results that were satisfactory for the model.

3.2.5.3 Alhazmi and Malaiya effort (AME) model

The calendar time interval is typically used by VDMs to make their predictions of vulnerabilities. Because of this, it is simpler to document the data on the vulnerabilities and relate them to a time span that has been normalized. On the other hand, this does not consider the effect of other factors, which might affect the vulnerability identification process. In order to explain the process of vulnerability identification, Alhazmi and Malaiya suggested an effort-based model. This model considers the influence that the user base of a product has. They reasoned that the proportion of a software's market share that corresponds to the number of installs of that software should be evaluated. Accordingly, it is reasonable to anticipate that a bigger number of users (efforts) will go into identifying vulnerabilities in a software system that has a higher user base (Alhazmi & Malaiya, 2005b). They referred to the effort as equivalent effort *(E)*, which may be computed using the following formula:

$$E = \sum_{i=0}^{n} (U_i \times P_i), \tag{3.19}$$

where U_i denotes the total number of users present at a time point and P_i is the market share of the software system under study. They considered that the vulnerability discovery with respect to effort applied at time t is directly proportional to the number of undiscovered vulnerabilities. The mathematical model can be given as

$$\Omega(E) = N\left(1 - e^{-rE}\right). \tag{3.20}$$

The model given in eqn (3.20) is analogous to the model proposed by Rescorla as given in eqn (3.16).

3.2.5.4 Kapur et al. (2015) logistic model

In contrast to the model suggested by Alhazmi and Malaiya's logistic model, the S-shaped model proposed by Kapur *et al.* makes use of the logistic discovery rate as an alternate formulation. This model was developed by Kapur *et al.* considered that the learning phenomena of the detector governs the discovery process, and as a result, they employed the logistic function in order to identify any previously unknown vulnerabilities that were present in the system.

The differential equation proposed by Kapur et al., (2015) describing the given scenario can be modeled as follows:

$$\frac{d\Omega(t)}{dt} = \frac{r}{1 + \beta e^{-rt}} \left(N - \Omega(t)\right), \tag{3.21}$$

where r is the rate of vulnerability discovery and the parameter β denotes the learning phenomenon of the detectors that attribute the shape of the curve. After solving eqn (3.21), using the initial condition $\Omega(0) = 0$, a closed form solution can be obtained as

$$\Omega(t) = N\left(\frac{1 - e^{-rt}}{1 + \beta e^{-rt}}\right). \tag{3.22}$$

The model proposed by Kapur et al., (2015) is flexible in nature, as it can express both S-shaped ($\beta > 1$) and exponential ($\beta = 0$) behaviors of the vulnerability discovery curve.

3.2.5.5 Other literature

In the realm of vulnerability discovery modeling, a wide variety of models, including the exponential and logistic models, as well as others, have been presented. According to Joh *et al.*, the process of discovering vulnerabilities follows an asymmetrical pattern. This is in contrast to the conventional S-shaped models, in which the noncumulative curve is symmetric and has a peak in the middle of it. Younis et al., (2011) used the folded normal distribution to simulate the vulnerability identification process in situations where there was either a shorter or nonexistent learning period. According to Younis, Joh, and Malaiya (2011), the nature of the suggested model is asymmetrical as well. In a separate piece of research, Joh *et al.* (2014) investigated the skewness that was present in the vulnerability datasets by considering a number of distribution functions, including the Weibull, beta, gamma, and normal distributions (Joha & Malaiya, 2014). In the event that there is more than one version of software on the market, it was also suggested that multiple-version VDMs be utilized as a method for combating the discovery phenomena. Kim, Malaiya, and Ray (2007) came up with the idea of proposing a generalized version of the AML model to describe the phenomena of numerous versions. In a similar vein, Anand et al., (2016) introduced a multi-version vulnerability detection model by taking into consideration simultaneous equations expressing the vulnerability count in each version (Anand et al., 2017). This model was developed by considering simultaneous equations representing the vulnerability count in each version.

3.2.6 Usefulness of VDMs

VDMs have the potential to improve the reliability of software security evaluations by delivering valuable quantitative measurements of vulnerabilities. In particular, VDMs may be put to use to make predictions about and comparisons between the various patterns of vulnerabilities found in software systems. The following is a list of some of the benefits that using VDMs can bring:

- assisting software companies in better understanding the latest security developments;
- providing an estimate of the total number of fixes that will need to be installed;

- assisting suppliers in allocating resources in accordance with the findings of the discovery pattern;
- coming up with an estimate for the typical amount of time until another vulnerability is found;
- evaluating comparable software applications.

The possible number of vulnerabilities in a piece of software enables a provider to accurately estimate the amount of time and resources needed to maintain the software system. In addition, the vendor is able to more accurately predict the number of patches necessary to correct the vulnerabilities. A vendor can more accurately estimate the amount of time necessary for the creation of patches and schedule the deployment of patches with the assistance of the MTTNV. As an illustration, Microsoft began to consistently schedule the delivery of security updates for its products on the second or sometimes fourth Tuesday of every month. This practice, which was subsequently dubbed "Patch Tuesday" in October 2003 (Budd, 2013), was one of the first instances of the term.

The VDMs are also helpful in calculating the amount of time necessary to remedy the vulnerabilities that have not been published. For instance, vendors may develop an assurance objective to plan the delivery of fixes based upon the expected timeline predicted using the vulnerabilities that have not yet been found. This goal may be used to track progress toward the target. They might be useful for comparing and quantifying the software security, which would benefit both consumers and providers. Users may seek to differentiate between two products by analyzing the fraction of remaining vulnerabilities or the rate at which vulnerabilities are discovered. One of the most significant metrics of software security is the discovery rate. A lower discovery rate suggests that vulnerabilities are not being exploited as quickly. The ability to foresee how their own project would behave in the field is another advantage for suppliers who compare their work to other projects with comparable characteristics.

Last but not least, VDMs may also be utilized by vendors in the process of allocating monies for the purpose of awarding prizes to detectors through a variety of bug bounty programs. Users are also incentivized to identify flaws and adhere to a disclosure policy in order to reduce the possibility that the vulnerabilities they find will be exploited. The program makes it possible for a vendor to protect themselves against the occurrence of breaches and exploits. When it comes to preventing a catastrophic breach of security, having an accurate count of the number of potential vulnerabilities that may come up in the future is helpful in allocating resources for the various sorts of programs involved.

3.3 Model validation

The majority of VDMs that exist are expressed by non-linear functions. To estimate the parameters of the models, two widely known techniques are used such as: non-linear least square (NLLS) and maximum likelihood estimation (MLE) (Kapur et al., 2011). The non-linear regression technique is generally used when the variables under study are related to each other in a random manner. However, when the mathematical equations under study are not simultaneous in nature, the NLLS technique is used. In this book, almost all the discussed mathematical functions are shown using the NLLS method.

Under the NLLS technique, the unknown parameters are obtained by minimizing the sum of least squares, i.e., the sum of squared deviations between the actual and predicted values of the model. To perform the computational work, various software tools such as IBM SPSS Statistics, SAS, etc. can be utilized, and thereby the unknown parameters can be deduced.

Thus, VDMs are mathematically comparable to SRGMs available in the literature (Massacci & Nguyen, 2014). It is possible that not every SRGM will properly capture the fault behavior of every project, but according to Farr, (1996), the vast majority of software projects can be accurately modeled by at least one SRGM. This is similar to the situation with software reliability. As a result, it is reasonable to anticipate that it will hold true for VDMs (Musa et al., 1987). The security practitioners may evaluate a model by fitting it to the observed dataset and likely to discover several goodness of fit metrics to compare the model's prediction capabilities. Verifying that the goodness of fit of a VDM falls within an acceptable range is the first step in determining whether or not it is capable of making accurate predictions. There are many different methods of testing that may be used to evaluate how well a model fits the data. The chi-square test (χ^2), the Akaike information criterion (AIC) test, the coefficient of determination test (R-squared), and other similar tests are some of the most applicable methods of testing. In spite of this, the prediction accuracy of a model is often regarded to be the most important test. The accuracy of a model's predictions may be evaluated using a variety of methods, some of which are described in more detail below.

- **Mean squared error (MSE)**: The mean square error can be defined as "the average squared difference between the expected values and the observed values." The MSE indicates the quality of an estimator, and the values closer to zero signify fewer fitting errors and are considered a better fit (Lehmann, 1998). MSE can be calculated as

$$\text{MSE} = \sum_{i=1}^{k} \frac{\left(\widehat{\Omega}\,(t_i) - \Omega(t_i)\right)^2}{k-p}, \tag{3.23}$$

where k is the number of time points and p is the number of parameters in the model.

- **Prediction error (PE)**: The prediction error represents "the difference between the actual and predicted values at any instant of time." Lower value of PE signifies a better fit. The behavior of prediction error can be evaluated using bias and variation. Bias is the average of PE. It depicts how far the actual values of the model are away from the average. And the variation resembles "how much the estimates varies around its average." The models having lower values of bias and variation advocate a better goodness of fit (Kapur et al., 2011).

$$\text{Bias} = \sum_{i=1}^{k} \frac{\left(\widehat{\Omega}\,(t_i) - \Omega(t_i)\right)}{k} \tag{3.24}$$

$$\text{Variation} = \sqrt{\left(\frac{1}{N-1}\right)\sum (\text{PE}_i - \text{Bias})^2}. \tag{3.25}$$

- **Root mean square prediction error (RMSPE)**: It is "a measure of closeness with which a model predicts the observation" (Kapur et al., 2011). RMSPE can be calculated as

$$\text{RMSPE} = \sqrt{\left(\text{Bias}^2 - \text{Variation}^2\right)}. \tag{3.26}$$

Lower the value of RMSPE, better the model fits the observed data.

- **Coefficient of determination (R^2)**: It is defined as "the ratio of the sum of squares (SS) resulting from the trend model to that from a constant model subtracted from 1." It represents how well the model predicts the values to approximate the actual values. The value of R^2 closer to 1 indicates a better fit (Kapur et al., 2011). It is given as

$$R^2 = 1 - \frac{\text{residual SS}}{\text{corrected SS}}. \tag{3.27}$$

- **Prediction-ratio risk (PRR)**: The PRR can be defined mathematically as (Sharma et al., 2010)

$$\mathrm{PRR} = \sum_{i=1}^{k} \frac{\left(\widehat{\Omega}\,(t_i) - \Omega(t_i)\right)}{\widehat{\Omega}(t_i)}. \tag{3.28}$$

- **Mean error of prediction (MEOP)**: It can be defined as "the sum of absolute value of the deviation between the observed value and the estimated value" (Sharma et al., 2010):

$$\mathrm{MEOP} : \sum_{i=1}^{k} \frac{\left|\widehat{\Omega}\,(t_i) - \Omega(t_i)\right|}{k - p + 1}. \tag{3.29}$$

- **Theil statistics (TS)**: It is defined as "the deviation percentage over all periods with respect to the actual observed values" (Sharma et al., 2010). The values that are closer to zero indicate a better fit of the model. It can be calculated as

$$\mathrm{TS} = \sqrt{\frac{\sum_{i=1}^{k} \left(\widehat{\Omega}\,(t_i) - \Omega(t_i)\right)^2}{\sum_{i=1}^{k} \left(\Omega(\mathrm{t}_i)\right)^2}}. \tag{3.30}$$

References

Lyu, M. R. (1996). *Handbook of Software Reliability Engineering.* USA: McGraw-Hill

Massacci, F., & Nguyen, V. H. (2014). An Empirical Methodology to Evaluate Vulnerability Discovery Models. *IEEE Transactions on Software Engineering*, 40(12), 1147-1162.

Needham, R. (2002). Security and open source. *Open Source Software.*

Alhazmi, O. H., & Malaiya, Y. K. (2005a). Modeling the vulnerability discovery process. *Proceedings of the 16th IEEE International Symposium on Software Reliability Engineering (ISSRE'05)* (pp. 129-138). Washington, DC, USA: IEEE Computer Society. Retrieved from https://www.cs.colostate.edu/~malaiya/pub/issre05.pdf

Gopalakrishna, R., & Spafford, E. H. (2005). *A Trend Analysis of Vulnerabilities.* West Lafayette, Indiana: CERIAS, Purdue University. Retrieved from https://www.cerias.purdue.edu/tools_and_resources/bibtex_archive/archive/2005-05.pdf

Ozment, A. (2007). Vulnerability Discovery & Software Security. *Ph.D. Dissertation.* Cambridge, UK.: University of Cambridge Computer Laboratory.

Rescorla, E. (2005). Is finding security holes a good idea? *IEEE Security & Privacy*, 3(1), 14-19

Kapur, P. K., Sachdeva, N., & Khatri, S. K. (2015). Vulnerability Discovery Modeling. *International conference on quality, reliability, infocom technology and industrial technology management*, (pp. 34-54). New Delhi.

Younis, A. A., Joh, H., & Malaiya, Y. K. (2011). Modeling Learningless Vulnerability Discovery using a Folded Distribution. *International Conference on Security and Management*, (pp. 617-623).

Joha, H., & Malaiya, Y. K. (2014). Modeling Skewness in Vulnerability Discovery. *Quality & Reliability Engineering International*, 30(8), 1445-1459.

Kim, J., Malaiya, Y. K., & Ray, I. (2007). Vulnerability Discovery in Multi-Version Software Systems. *10th IEEE High Assurance Systems Engineering Symposium* (pp. 141-148). Plano, TX, USA: IEEE.

Anand, A., & Bhatt, N. (2016). Vulnerability discovery modeling and weighted criteria based ranking. Journal of the Indian Society for Probability and Statistics, 17, 1-10.

Anand, A., Das, S., Aggrawal, D., & Klochkov, Y. (2017). Vulnerability Discovery Modelling for Software with Multi-versions. In M. Ram, & J. P. Davim, *Advances in Reliability and System Engineering* (pp. 255-265). Cham: Springer

Budd, C. (2013, October 31). *Ten Years of Patch Tuesdays: Why It's Time to Move On*. Retrieved from GeekWire: https://www.geekwire.com/2013/ten-years-patch-tuesdays-time-move/.

Kapur, P. K., Pham, H., Jha, P., & Gupta, A. (2011). *Software Reliability Assessment with OR Applications.* London: Springer.

https://vulners.com/securityvulns/SECURITYVULNS:DOC:6319

Farr, W. (1996). Software Reliability Modeling Survey. In M. R. Lyu, *Handbook of Software Reliability Engineering* (pp. 71-117). McGraw-Hill.

Musa, J. D., Iannino, A., & Okumoto, K. (1987). *Software Reliability: Measurement, Prediction, Application.* New York, NY, USA: McGraw-Hill.

Lehmann, E. L. (1998). *Theory of Point Estimation.* New York: Springer.

Sharma, K., Garg, R., Nagpal, C., & Garg, R. (2010). Selection of optimal software reliability growth models using a distance based approach. *IEEE Transactions on Reliability*, 59(2), 266-276.

4

Vulnerability Discovery Models based on Calendar Time

Many different sorts of human activities may now be performed automatically because of the software solutions that have been developed and built. It is impossible to rule out the chance of software malfunctions occurring throughout the time that these systems are in use, despite the fact that the developer of software systems is the most powerful and smartest being in the universe. The creators of these products are mostly to blame for the flaws that have been manifested in their products. Software testing is done with the primary intention of locating and fixing the majority of the underlying issues that have been found. In spite of the fact that the software testing and debugging team puts in a lot of effort, employs a variety of methods, engineering techniques, well-planned, and controlled strategies, and even though the developers spend a lot of money on testing and debugging, we cannot guarantee that the software will be free of any and all flaws when it is released. This is because the software testing and debugging team uses distinct methods, engineering techniques, and well-planned and controlled strategies.

The only way that seems feasible for software engineers is to have a preplanned estimation of vulnerabilities that will be discovered in due course of time. And, the VDMs provide a best fit to measure that information and can help a software engineer to cater the necessary resources and provide timely patches for the vulnerabilities yet to be discovered. This chapter provides a detailed overview of various vulnerability discovery models that can be used to model the discovery phenomenon by considering various patterns in which a vulnerability is discovered in a software system.

To acquaint the readers how the VDMs are applied to the real-life setting, we first discuss the type of data we use to evaluate the prediction capability of VDMs. Thus, the VDMs work on the historical data of vulnerabilities that were disclosed in the various vulnerability repositories. One example of this kind of database is called the National Vulnerability Database (NVD), and it is kept up to date by the National Institute of Standards and Technology (NIST). The NVD is the principal database that is consulted for any and all analyses concerning VDMs. However, it was not intended to be utilized in the vulnerability discovery modeling. Instead, the NVD employees are tasked with analyzing the common vulnerabilities and exposures (CVEs) by obtaining data points from a variety of public platforms, such as vendor advisory reports and third-party institutions, amongst other examples. The research also supplies additional security metrics associated with vulnerabilities, such as the common vulnerability scoring system (CVSS) and the common weakness enumeration (CWE), in addition to other pertinent data. More than a hundred thousand entries relating to CVEs that have been published by a variety of software manufacturers or obtained from public platforms make up the NVD. Each entry in the CVE database has its own unique identifier (ID), a CVSS score, a vulnerability category, a CWE ID, information on the product and the manufacturer, and a brief written description of the vulnerability. In addition to that, various links to external websites containing further information about a vulnerability are also supplied. In addition, several links pertaining to information on exploits associated with a vulnerability are provided. If there is a known exploit for a vulnerability, the details about that exploit will also be published. However, a large number of links will need to be updated in due course since, in many instances, information on the availability of patches and exploits was not readily available at the time that the vulnerability was disclosed.

The historical data from CVE needs to be converted into data based on calendar time so that it can show the number of vulnerabilities that are found or disclosed in a particular time period. Then, a mathematical model needs to be evaluated based on the per-unit-time data in order to determine the vulnerabilities that are going to be found in the future according to the pattern that has been established by the behavior of the system in the past. The trend that is being explored by many researchers in the literature gives a software engineer the ability to pick from a variety of sets of models that will properly fit with the vulnerabilities detected in a software system when it is in its operational phase.

4.1 Calendar Time Models

The vast majority of proposed VDMs in the literature employ calendar time since it is the time component that has the most relevance to software developers, designers, and end users. In this chapter, we begin our discussion with the calendar time models, which were initially introduced in this category. Additionally, we describe the vulnerability discovery models employed in this chapter, which are concave and S-shaped models. The Rescorla exponential model, which was first developed in 2005, is regarded as an important pioneering effort. Models that were developed later primarily aimed to integrate more components of the discovery process while also attempting to loosen some assumptions made by the model.

Following are the notations that have been used while modeling the vulnerability discovery process:

$\Omega(t)$: Cumulative number of vulnerabilities discovered by time t.
N: Total number of vulnerabilities present in the software system.
r: Vulnerability discovery rate.
β: Parameter to depict the learning of detectors.

4.1.1 Rescorla exponential model

Eric Rescorla made the initial suggestion for a VDM in the year 2005. In their approach, the vulnerability detection rate is derived directly from the actual data. They developed an estimate for the total number of software flaws by employing the aforementioned data in conjunction with the conventional procedures for ensuring the reliability of software. Their method was quite similar to the Goel–Okumoto reliability model, and it was used to match empirical data on the rate of vulnerability discovery, which allowed them to derive the total number of vulnerabilities. Additionally, the model provides a projection of the vulnerability discovery rate through time and, as a result, the chance of vulnerability discovery at any given moment. In addition, the software only goes through a single release and the software is released with a fixed number of vulnerabilities. During the course of the software's existence, some flaws were found, and patches were developed to address them. If we assume that such fixes never result in the introduction of new vulnerabilities, then the general quality of the software will steadily improve. Because of this, the software will be less susceptible to vulnerabilities subsequently, and the system will be seen as more trustworthy.

In the context of this discussion, Rescorla considers that the reliability is defined as the number of failures or vulnerabilities that are observed over the course of a specific amount of time. If a system is shown to be becoming more reliable, then this indicates that it is experiencing fewer instances of failure or vulnerabilities. The model, in the interest of simplicity, assumes that the consequences of all failures are the same. Rescorla considered that the vulnerabilities are being identified at an exponential rate but at a consistent rate. The Poisson process features were utilized by Rescorla in order to account for the amount of vulnerabilities found in a software per unit of time. According to Rescorla (2005), the model assumed that the number of vulnerabilities revealed at any given time point or the vulnerability intensity is proportionate to the total number of vulnerabilities that are still to be detected. That is, the total value that may be predicted from a Poisson process is directly proportional to the number of unknown flaws at the time t. As a consequence of this, the curve representing the predicted value follows an exponential decay. Mathematically, the vulnerability discovery rate can be illustrated using the differential equation as follows:

$$\frac{d\Omega(t)}{dt} \propto (N - \Omega(t)). \tag{4.1}$$

The discovery of vulnerabilities will occur, at a predetermined rate r, to identify any remaining flaws that have not yet been found. The differential equation that was presented in eqn (4.1) may also be represented as

$$\frac{d\Omega(t)}{dt} = r(N - \Omega(t)). \tag{4.2}$$

The solution of eqn (4.2) can be found using the initial condition, $\Omega(0) = 0$. A closed form of eqn (4.2) can be written as

$$\Omega(t) = N\left(1 - e^{-rt}\right). \tag{4.3}$$

The model is known as Rescorla exponential model as it describes an exponential vulnerability discovery curve. The model has been applied to various vulnerability datasets, and in a number of situations, it provides a good estimation and prediction. However, the discovery pattern undertaken by most of the recent software systems incorporate learning phenomenon that results an unstable fit for Rescorla model on the recent datasets. To acknowledge this behavior, other models considering different discovery patterns were later proposed and are discussed in the next section.

4.1.2 Alhazmi and Malaiya logistic (AML) model

Following the exponential model, another group of researchers at Colorado State University have been investigating the use of VDMs. Alhazmi and Malaiya came up with the idea that would later become known as the AML model. The model assumed that the discovery pattern would evolve into an

S-shaped (logistic) pattern over the course of time. Unlike Rescorla, they consider that as the software is released to the general public, the vulnerability discovery pattern follows a specific pattern that incorporates learning, linear and saturation stages, and can be visualized as an S-shaped pattern.

The idea behind developing this model was the pattern in which vulnerabilities were reported in Windows 95, Windows 98, and Windows XP. Thus, all the Windows operating systems shared similar modules, and the majority of vulnerabilities were shared by all of the releases. In their study, they found that Windows 95 demonstrated gradual expansion at first, up until about March 1998. After that point, it reached a point of saturation, which lasted for many months. Similar to Windows 95, Windows 98 saw rather sluggish growth until about June 1998. Thereafter, the expansion of Windows 95 and Windows 98 operating systems accelerated. Because of the striking similarities between these operating systems, it appears that Windows 98 and Windows 95 shared a sizeable portion of their respective source codes. The number of computers running Windows 98 reached its highest point during the years 1999 and 2000. After this point in time, the rates at which vulnerabilities were discovered in both versions of the software began to decrease. Windows 95 demonstrates a greater degree of the saturation. Based on the observations of common vulnerabilities, a significant number of flaws in Windows 95 that were found at a later date were, in fact, identified in the Windows 98 release. It would appear that the number of cumulative security holes in Windows 95 and Windows 98 has reached a point of stability. The existence of some holes in Windows 98 was not uncovered until much later. The underlying reason for this is the code that was shared between the Windows 98 and Windows XP versions, which will be covered in the following section.

When compared to the date of its release, it was found that Windows XP showed a rapid increase in the number of vulnerabilities. Additionally, there were a large number of vulnerabilities that were shared with Windows 98. XP does, however, have its own special vulnerabilities, and they make up the vast bulk of them. Instead, the figure demonstrates a linear accumulation of vulnerabilities, which is consistent with Windows XP's lack of a distinct learning phase. In their work, it can be seen that the Windows 98 operating system has demonstrated a more drawn-out learning phase, which is then followed by linear accumulation and, finally, saturation. As a consequence of this, it would appear that Windows XP was responsible for the discovery of the majority of the vulnerabilities that were present in subsequent versions of Windows 98. The findings for the three different versions of the operating system show that there is a strong dependency between the vulnerability detection rates for each of the versions.

The discovery pattern of vulnerabilities shown in different operation systems of Microsoft resulted in three phases, which signifies the different stages of vulnerability discovery phenomenon, i.e., learning, linear, and saturation and can be shown in Figure 4.1.

The usage environment is subject to change across these three phases, which in turn has an effect on the vulnerability identification effort. The initial part shows a flat portion of the curve. In this case, following the introduction of a software, the detectors require time to learn about the software; as a consequence, there were fewer reports of vulnerabilities. The detectors have started to get an understanding of the software and have started to collect sufficient information linked to any potential gaps that may exist in the software. The next segment of the curve, which is steeper, can be used to describe this stage. Detectors are now familiar with the software, and they understand how the software works; as a result, there has been an increase in the number of vulnerabilities that have been reported by the detector. In addition, the vast majority of users have consented to use the software, and its level of popularity has reached an all-time high. At this time, vulnerability

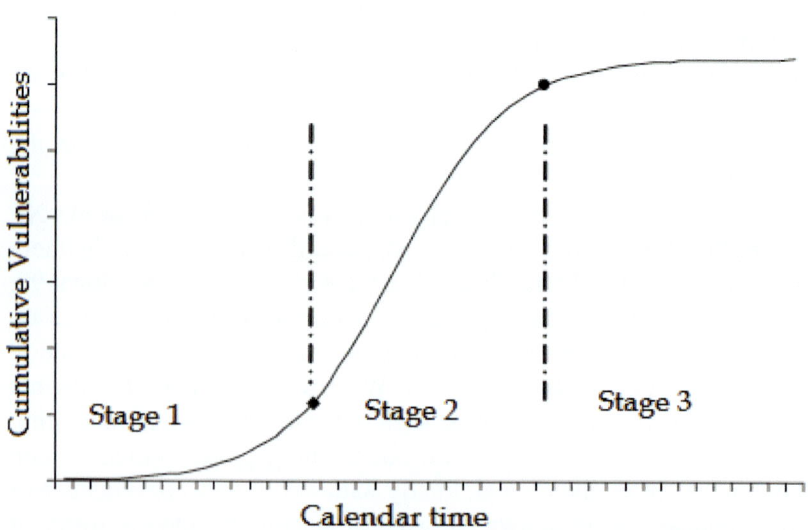

Figure 4.1 The three-stages of the vulnerability discovery process (Source: Alhazmi & Malaiya 2005).

detectors are likely to receive the greatest rewards. After that point, the discovery process reaches a plateau, which is represented by the segment of the curve that is flat. The majority of users have upgraded to a more recent version of the software, which has resulted in a fall in the discovery rate as well as a reduction in the number of vulnerability detection instances.

Here, the discovery phenomenon is depicted by two factors that govern the rate at which vulnerabilities are discovered. The first of them is because of the momentum obtained by the market acceptance of the product, which is represented by a factor $r\Omega(t)$, where r is a proportionality constant. The second of these is because of the success of the product. The second component is saturation, which arises from the fact that there are a finite number of vulnerabilities. This factor is proportional to $(N - \Omega(t)))$.

Following is the differential equation to depict the behavior of vulnerability discovery process at which vulnerabilities are discovered:

$$\frac{d\Omega(t)}{dt} = r\Omega\left(t\right)\left(N - \Omega\left(t\right)\right). \tag{4.4}$$

The solution of eqn (4.4) can be given as

$$\Omega\left(t\right) = \frac{N}{1 + NCe^{-rNt}}, \tag{4.5}$$

where N, r, and C are the parameters of the model representing the total number of vulnerabilities, vulnerability discovery rate, and constant introduced while solving eqn (4.5), respectively. The suggested model was evaluated on a variety of software encompassing a wide range of software classes. The software included browsers, Linux and Windows operating systems, and more. The majority of the datasets had chi-square goodness of fit results that were satisfactory for the model.

4.1.3 Asymmetric folded VDM

A software system will often change over time as bugs are fixed, patches are applied, and new features are implemented. This will introduce fresh vulnerabilities into the system, putting off saturation for longer. Many people will upgrade to a new version as soon as it becomes available. The time required to learn anything new will consequently decrease, if not vanish entirely. When the learning phase is very small, then to model the discovery process, Younis et.al. (2011) proposed a folded VDM.

The normal distribution is specified for a random variable that can take on values ranging from $-\infty$ to $+\infty$, and it has a symmetrical shape around its mean. In some circumstances, a distribution that does not contain any negative numbers is required. Daniel had suggested a distribution called a half-normal distribution, which folds the normal distribution at the mean, which at this time corresponds to the value zero. Leone *et al.* came up with a more generalized form of it, which they referred to as a folded normal distribution. This distribution is defined for a random variable that may take on values between 0 and $+\infty$. It is created by including the values that are negative on the side of the distribution that is positive. A folded distribution will always be the one that is obtained when measurements of a regularly distributed random variable have been collected, despite the fact that the algebraic sign has been disregarded in the process. It has been discovered that the folded distribution may be utilized in a variety of industrial practices, including the measuring of flatness and the straightening and calculation of the center of the sprocket holes in motion picture film. Both the probability density function (PDF) and the cumulative distribution function (CDF) of the distribution may be derived from the normal distribution.

Folded VDM either has a shorter learning phase or none at all, which results in an asymmetrical normal distribution. It leads to a greater discovery rate at the beginning, which may be particularly useful in the circumstances when the vulnerability discovery is linear even at the beginning of the process.

The vulnerability discovery begins at time $t = 0$, which corresponds to the time the software was released. The learning period is cut down significantly due to the fact that the beginning value is not zero as a result of the contribution of folding. The following equation can be used to indicate the rate at which vulnerabilities are being discovered.

$$\omega\left(t\right)=\frac{N}{\sqrt{2\pi}\sigma}\left[e^{-\left(\frac{(t-\tau)^2}{2\sigma^2}\right)}+e^{-\left(\frac{(t+\tau)^2}{2\sigma^2}\right)}\right],\ t\geq 0, \tag{4.6}$$

where σ and τ represent a scale and location parameter, respectively. The portion of the distribution that is folded to the positive side is represented by the second term in the equation. Similarly, the cumulative number of vulnerabilities discovered by time t is presented in the below equation:

$$\Omega\left(t\right)=\frac{N}{\sqrt{2\pi}\sigma}\left[\mathrm{erf}\left(\frac{(t-\tau)}{\sqrt{2}\sigma}\right)+\mathrm{erf}\left(\frac{(t+\tau)}{\sqrt{2}\sigma}\right)\right],\ t\geq 0, \tag{4.7}$$

where $\mathrm{erf}()$ is the error function that is used to calculate the integral from zero.

4.1.4 Normal distribution based VDM

The normal distribution, also known as the Gaussian distribution, is a continuous probability distribution that is used in statistics to describe a dataset that tends to congregate around an anticipated value. It is a symmetrical distribution, and there is no skewness to speak of, much like the AML model. It has a form that is comparable to the logistic distribution that the AML model uses, but the tails on both sides are less extreme.

The probability density function (PDF) for the normal distribution and logistic distribution is shown in Figure 4.2. It can be seen that in the normal distribution, the dataset bunches around the expected value and also it has a long tail where there are a small number of incidences of events under observation. However, in case of logistic distribution, the dataset also groups around the mean but it has a heavy tail with higher probabilities in the tails. Therefore, if a vulnerability dataset has fewer incidences at the beginning and at the end of a discovery process, then the normal distribution based VDM may perform better than the logistic distribution based model.

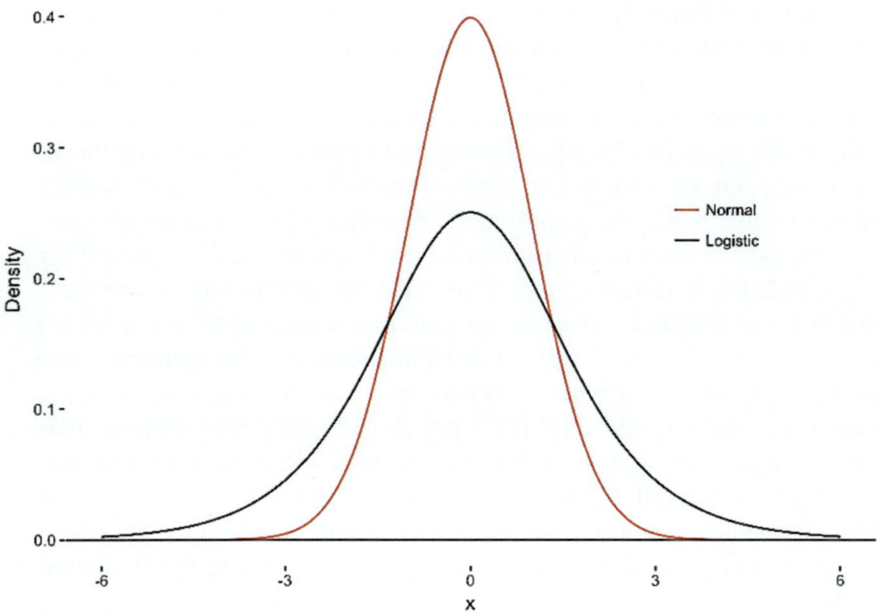

Figure 4.2 Probability density function (PDF) of normal and logistic distribution (Source: Kapur et.al., 2011).

When the initial and ending vulnerability occurrences in a software system are few, then the vulnerability intensity rate can be represented using the following equation:

$$\omega(t) = \frac{Ne^{-\frac{(t-\mu)}{s}}}{s\left(1+e^{-\frac{(t-\mu)}{s}}\right)^2},\ t \geq 0, \tag{4.8}$$

where σ and μ represent scale and location parameters, respectively. The cumulative number of vulnerabilities to be discovered by time t can be given by

$$\Omega(t) = \frac{N}{1+e^{-\frac{(t-\mu)}{s}}}. \tag{4.9}$$

In eqn (4.9), as the t becomes closer and closer to infinity, then the right-hand side will converge to N. As a result, N is a representation of the overall number of vulnerabilities that will eventually be found in a software.

4.1.5 Gamma distribution based VDM

The Gamma distribution is a type of continuous probability distribution that has two parameters: a shape parameter denoted by the symbol and a scale parameter denoted by the symbol. The only t values for which this distribution can be specified are those ranging from zero to positive infinity. It occurs naturally in processes in which the waiting times between Poisson distributed events are relevant. For instance, in life testing, the waiting time until death is a random variable that is frequently modeled using the Gamma distribution. This is because the Gamma distribution is used as a probabilistic model for waiting times. For t values greater than zero, the distribution is specified. When a vulnerability dataset is right skewed, the Gamma distribution, which is a member of the family of right-skewed distributions, may perform more effectively than other distributions. When time t is sufficiently large, many datasets describing vulnerability discovery should seem right-skewed. This is because the number of vulnerabilities discovered will eventually decrease, which will generate a tail on the right side of the curve.

The vulnerability intensity function for a software in which the discovery pattern follows Gamma distribution can be represented using the following equation:

$$\omega(t) = \frac{N}{\Gamma(\alpha)\beta^{\alpha}} t^{\alpha-1} e^{-\frac{t}{\beta}},\ t \geq 0 \tag{4.10}$$

$$\text{where } \Gamma(\alpha) = \int_0^\infty t^{\alpha-1} e^{-t} dt, \tag{4.11}$$

where α and β represent shape and scale parameters, respectively. The cumulative number of vulnerabilities to be discovered by time t can be given by

$$\Omega(t_0) = \int_{t=0}^{t_0} \frac{N}{\Gamma(\alpha)\beta^\alpha} t^{\alpha-1} e^{-\frac{t}{\beta}}. \tag{4.12}$$

Eqn 4.12 can be used to represent the corresponding cumulative vulnerabilities to be predicted using the model. As α increases, the Gamma distribution becomes more symmetrical.

4.1.6 Weibull distribution based VDM

In the field of reliability engineering, the Weibull distribution is one of the lifespan distributions that is utilized the most frequently. It has been demonstrated via empirical research by Li et.al. (2004) that the Weibull model is superior to other reliability models when it comes to the occurrence of defects in a wide variety of software systems (Li et.al., 2004). Zhou and Davis have demonstrated the applicability of the Weibull distribution to explain the failure process data from a variety of open source projects by fitting the distribution to time-related bug reporting patterns (Zhou & Davis, 2005).

In the case of exponential models, the software system demonstrates a declining vulnerability intensity function during the discovery process. This may be seen as an indication that there is an increase in the level of software security throughout the course of the vulnerability discovery process. In the vast majority of instances that occur in real life, the degree of vulnerability worsens at first but subsequently improves over the course of time. The Weibull distribution has been shown to be effective in capturing this phenomenon while adopting this behavior of growing and reducing vulnerability intensity due to the value of its shape parameter. This success may be attributed to the fact that the Weibull distribution has been shown to be successful.

The vulnerability intensity rate for a Weibull distribution based VDM can be represented using the following equation:

$$\omega(t) = N\frac{\alpha}{\beta}\left(\frac{t}{\beta}\right)^{\alpha-1} e^{-\left(\frac{t}{\beta}\right)^\alpha}. \tag{4.13}$$

The cumulative number of vulnerabilities to be discovered in a software can be represented as

$$\Omega\left(t\right) = N\left(1 - e^{-\left(\frac{t}{\beta}\right)^{\alpha}}\right). \tag{4.14}$$

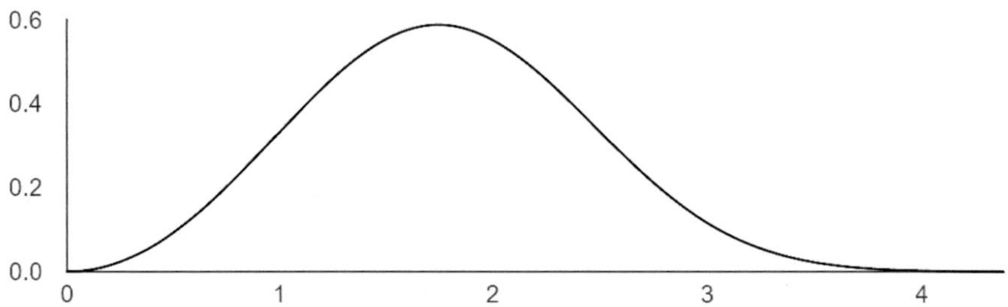

Figure 4.3 Shape of vulnerability discovery process when $\alpha\sim3$ (Source: Author's work).

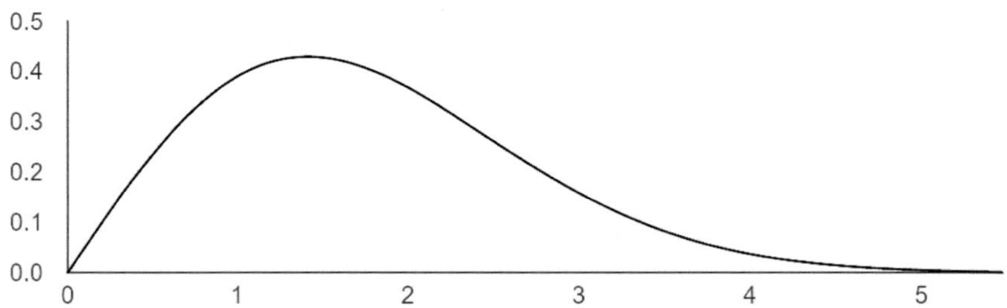

Figure 4.4 Shape of vulnerability discovery process when $\alpha<3$ (Source: Author's work).

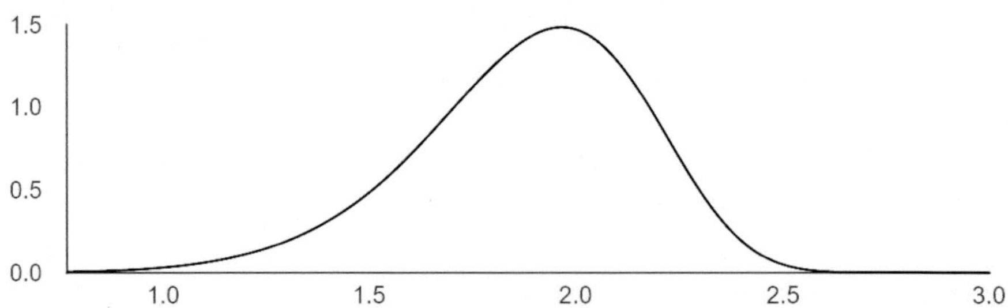

Figure 4.5 Shape of vulnerability discovery process when $\alpha>3$ (Source: Author's work).

In this case, the shape of the software vulnerability discovery process is determined by the value of α. When α is close to the value 3, the form is said to be symmetrical. When α is more than 3, the curve has a negative skewness, and when α is less than 3, the curve has a positive skewness. The length of time may be adjusted with the β parameter. Such behavior can be observed from Figures 4.3 till 4.5.

4.1.7 Kapur et al. (2015) logistic model

In contrast to the model suggested by Alhazmi and Malaiya's logistic model, the S-shaped model proposed by Kapur *et al.* makes use of the logistic discovery rate as an alternate formulation. They believe that the learning phenomena of the detector govern the discovery process, and as a result, they employed the logistic function to capture the unknown vulnerabilities that were present in the system (Kapur et.al., 2015). This was done because they feel that the learning phenomenon of the reporter is the governing factor in the discovery process. The differential equation that Kapur et.al. (2015) suggested can be used to describe the situation in question that may be modeled as follows:

$$\frac{d\Omega(t)}{dt} = \frac{r}{1+\beta e^{-rt}}\left(N - \Omega(t)\right), \tag{4.15}$$

where r is the rate of vulnerability discovery and the parameter β denotes the learning phenomenon of the detectors that attribute the shape of the curve. After solving eqn (4.15), using the initial condition $\Omega(0) = 0$, a closed form solution can be obtained as

$$\Omega(t) = N\left(\frac{1-e^{-rt}}{1+\beta e^{-rt}}\right). \tag{4.16}$$

The model proposed by Kapur et.al. (2015) is flexible in nature, as it can express both S-shaped ($\beta > 1$) and exponential ($\beta = 0$) behavior of the vulnerability discovery curve.

4.1.8 Hump-shaped model

When compared to the process of testing software, the discovery process involves a significantly larger number of detectors. And the bulk of the detectors that are used in the process of detecting any vulnerability are heavily affected either by the benefits that are linked with finding a vulnerability or by trying to exploit the vulnerabilities. In addition, the desirability of the program contributes to an increase in the number of users who select to make use of it. To put it more precisely, each new version of software has the potential to draw a growing number of detectors throughout the early portion of its lifecycle since more people are using it. When the maximum number of detectors is reached, the program gradually loses its appeal over time since more detectors are upgrading to more recent versions of the software. As a direct result of this, there would be a reduction in the number of vulnerabilities discovered. As a result, it is reasonable to predict that the rate of vulnerability discovery follows a curve with a humped form. Derivative of the logistic function can be used to mathematically describe this feature of the vulnerability detection rate, which may be obtained by

$$r\left(t\right)=\left(\frac{r^{2}\beta e^{-rt}}{\left(1+\beta e^{-rt}\right)^{2}}\right). \tag{4.17}$$

The differential equation given in eqn (4.17) can be further written as

$$\frac{d\Omega(t)}{dt}=\left(\frac{r^{2}\beta e^{-rt}}{\left(1+\beta e^{-rt}\right)^{2}}\right)\left(N-\Omega(t)\right). \tag{4.18}$$

Solving eqn (4.18) under the initial condition $\Omega\left(t=0\right)=0$, we can obtain the cumulative number of vulnerabilities to be discovered by time *t* as

$$\Omega\left(t\right)=N\left(1-e^{-r\left\{\left(\frac{1}{1+\beta e^{-rt}}\right)-\left(\frac{1}{1+\beta}\right)\right\}}\right). \tag{4.19}$$

It is interesting to note the behavior of the proposed model. Initially, when the vulnerability discovery process begins, i.e., at $t=0$, $\Omega\left(t=0\right)=0$ and at later stages when the vulnerability discovery process is carried on for an infinite time, i.e., at $t=\infty$, the vulnerabilities are almost discovered and can be given as

$$\Omega\left(t=\infty\right)=N\left(1-e^{-r\left(\frac{\beta}{1+\beta}\right)}\right). \tag{4.20}$$

4.2 Effort-based Models

VDMs have an influence on the correctness of the data when it comes to how accurate the data is when they are applied. As an illustration, software developers often choose the use of execution time rather than calendar time when working with SRGMs. However, because of the nature of the detection process, it might be difficult to collect correct chronological data for VDMs.

Many detectors in the detection process are external, meaning they are not hired by the vendor. As a consequence of this, it is difficult to correctly estimate the amount of work put in by detectors, as well as their number and their level of understanding.

Best practices for SRGM say that the amount of time on the calendar should be normalized based on the number of people testing the software system (Lyu, 1996). For illustration's sake, let us say Ram and Shyam collaborate for a week to uncover a security hole and then report their findings. If calendar time is normalized for the number of individuals, it may be deduced that this vulnerability was discovered after two weeks of work. One detector that is operational for two weeks is comparable to two detectors that are operational for one week.

It is possible that the truth is even more convoluted: Ram, an inexperienced detector, and Shyam, a highly proficient detector, worked variable hours and part time to find a weakness. The amount of effort that went into finding a vulnerability may be broken down into three components: the number of detectors, the level of expertise they possessed, and the total number of hours they put in. In a perfect world, vulnerability databases would also contain effort information, which could then be used to standardize the chronological information.

However, there is not a unique vulnerability database that has exact information regarding the amount of effort that was put into finding each vulnerability. The researchers Alhazmi and Malaiya suggest an effort-based model and claim that system user numbers should be used as a proxy for effort. However, there is little evidence to suggest that data on consumption is an appropriate substitute for the amount of effort put forward by detectors. There is no guarantee that a certain percentage of the entire user base is composed of individuals who are specifically interested in finding vulnerabilities. In addition, vulnerability detectors could choose to test software that is widely used in their community or that is receiving a lot of attention from the media at the moment. Because of this, the ratio of detectors to users might be different between programs and also change over time.

Since vulnerabilities are often identified by external detectors, it is highly unlikely that it will be possible to collect information that is both extensive and accurate regarding the effort that they put forth. So, the best that VDMs can do is model the finding process based on how vulnerability identification worked at the time the model was made. In the following subsection, we provide some mathematical models that consider effort data in identifying the vulnerabilities in a software.

4.2.1 Alhazmi and Malaiya effort (AME) based model

The calendar time interval is typically used by VDMs to make their predictions of vulnerabilities. Because of this, it is simpler to document the data on the vulnerabilities and relate them to a time span that has been normalized. On the other hand, this does not consider the effect of other factors, which might affect the vulnerability identification process. In order to explain the process of vulnerability identification, Alhazmi and Malaiya suggested an effort-based model. This model considers the influence that the user base of a product has. They reasoned that the proportion of a software's market share that corresponds to the number of installs of that software should be evaluated. Accordingly, it is reasonable to anticipate that a bigger number of users (efforts) will go into identifying vulnerabilities in a software system that has a higher user base (Alhazmi & Malaiya, 2005b). They referred to the effort as equivalent effort *(E)*, which may be computed using the following formula:

$$E = \sum_{i=0}^{n} (U_i \times P_i), \tag{4.21}$$

where U_i denotes the total number of users present at a time point and P_i is the market share of the software system under study. They considered that the vulnerability discovery with respect to effort applied at time t is directly proportional to the number of undiscovered vulnerabilities. The mathematical model can be given as

$$\Omega\,(E) = N\left(1 - e^{-rE}\right). \tag{4.22}$$

The model given in eqn (4.22) is analogous to the model proposed by Rescorla as given in eqn (4.3).

4.2.2 Reporter-based vulnerability discovery model

In this section of the book, a mathematical model for modeling the vulnerability discovery process for a software product on the basis of reporters reporting a vulnerability is discussed. The model is based on the fact that reporters report a vulnerability. According to Ozment, the amount of effort that went into finding a vulnerability is dependent on a variety of factors, including the capability of the researchers, the number of hours they put in, and the number of reporters they used (Ozment, 2007). According to Massacci & Nguyen (2014), software systems that have a larger market share are more appealing to attackers, and as a result, the number of users that utilize these systems grows over the course of time. It is presumed that the end users of the software systems are trustworthy individuals who can disclose flaws. There is frequently a correlation between the number of available detectors reporting a vulnerability and the vulnerabilities that are identified at a specific period. The discovery process that was modeled under the vulnerability environment based on time has been modeled differently than the discovery process that was modeled based on the behavior of detectors suggesting a discovery at any time point. If a larger number of people are actively searching for vulnerabilities and, as a result, influencing the discovery process, then there is a bigger chance that a vulnerability will be found. Moreover, the methodical framework will allow the software firms to evaluate the resources or external detectors required to accommodate the vulnerabilities discovery process throughout the software lifecycle.

An interdisciplinary and systematic strategy is necessary in order to blend the dynamic interaction of one system with another in order to derive a VDM that is based on the effect of reporters/detectors that indicate the vulnerabilities. Because of this, the investigation of a single system on its own could not produce the best results. It is possible that appropriate results can be obtained by combining two or more mathematical modeling techniques with one another. The number of real purchasers of a software product who report any bugs detected while using the program makes up the total number of reports for that software. To analyze the usage pattern in the growth of reporters who are reporting any defects observed in the operational phase, several diffusion models that are accessible in the marketing literature were used to simulate the situation. The intensity with which vulnerabilities are discovered during the operational use of a software is dependent on the number of reporters trying to find out the vulnerabilities. The behavior of reporters discovering a vulnerability plays an important role in the discovery process. Thus, the reporters are authentic buyers/users of a software and the growth rate of users of a software product varies with time. The user function so defined shows an increasing fashion in the beginning and then tailing off in the user rate. The drop in the user growth rate can be attributed due to the disinterest shown by the users about a software version (Kenny, 1993).

4.2.2.1 Notations

The notations used in the formulation of mathematical framework are as follows:

$\Omega, \Omega(t)$: Expected number of vulnerabilities discovered by time t.

$I,\ I(t)$: Expected number of vulnerability reports by time t.
$C(t)$: Counting process.
N : Total number of vulnerabilities present in the software system.
b : Coefficient describing the rate by which vulnerabilities are discovered.
β : Learning parameter.
α : Total number of reporters/detectors.

4.2.2.2 Model development

As previously mentioned in Chapter 1, the assumption is made that the vulnerability discovery function would follow an NHPP. As a result, the vulnerability intensity function during the operational stage of a program may be characterized as a function of time that is dependent on the reporters reporting a vulnerability. Thus, the underlying objective function is reliant on the usage function of reporters, which in turn is dependent on the passage of time. Therefore, by applying the chain rule of differentiation, the vulnerability intensity function may be thought of as the composite of the following two functions:

$$\frac{d\Omega(t)}{dt} = \frac{d\Omega(t)}{dI(t)} \cdot \frac{dI\,(t)}{dt}. \tag{4.23}$$

In the above expression, each component on the right-hand side of the differential equation is explicitly dependent upon I and t, respectively; however, these functions are indirectly time dependent on the same horizon. The number of vulnerabilities that are discovered increases as more software users adopt the software and reports the vulnerabilities with respect to the time. When more people start using the software and report security flaws, the likelihood that those flaws will be found grows, which in turn raises the number of vulnerabilities that are found.

The first component of eqn (4.23) relates the number of vulnerabilities discovered due to the influence of number of reporters reporting the vulnerabilities. The vulnerabilities that are identified during the operational stage by both in-house and external users and relevant fixes are provided at this time based on the impact these vulnerabilities have on the system. Ozment also emphasized the reliance in the process of discovering vulnerabilities, which involves the reporters finding more vulnerabilities when studying a previously reported vulnerability (Ozment, 2007). He talked about this dependency in the vulnerability detection process. Because of the conditions described above, a significant number of vulnerabilities can be uncovered in a very short amount of time, which was the initial step in the vulnerability discovery process. In addition, Alhazmi & Malaiya (2005a) and Kapur et.al. (2015) both promoted the influence of the learning phenomena of users in order to produce an S-shaped curve during the vulnerability identification process. In order to remedy the issue described above, the rate of vulnerabilities being discovered is modeled as an S-shaped logistic function for the purpose of simulating the effect of learning on vulnerability reports. The users, in the natural order of events, take some time to study the software system, and once they are familiar with the software, they are able to swiftly find flaws in the software. Last but not least, the procedure becomes less difficult as a result of individuals losing interest in locating them. As a result, the number of software vulnerabilities found to be the result of the reporters' actions at any given time *t* is directly related to the number of vulnerabilities that are still present in the software.

Hence, the first component of eqn (4.23) can be written as

$$\frac{d\Omega(t)}{dI(t)} = b\left(I(t)\right)\left(N - \Omega(t)\right), \tag{4.24}$$

where

$$b\left(I\left(t\right)\right) = \frac{b}{1 + \beta e^{-b \cdot I(t)}}. \tag{4.25}$$

Substituting eqn (4.25) in eqn (4.24), the following expression can be obtained:

$$\frac{d\Omega(t)}{dI(t)} = \frac{b}{1 + \beta e^{-b \cdot I(t)}}\left(N - \Omega(t)\right). \tag{4.26}$$

The expansion of reporters is considered in relation to the passage of time in the second part of eqn (4.23). After a piece of software has been made available to the wider public, its end users will adopt it, and a certain percentage of its genuine users will disclose vulnerabilities to the product's vendor. This particular behavior of reporters can be understood through what has been proposed in marketing science (Bass, 1969). It is possible to indicate the number of reports using the function *I(t)* at any time *t*. Now, when a piece of software is released to its customers, a certain percentage of end users will report security flaws, and this percentage of users will almost certainly alter over the course of time. Following is a mathematical representation of how this rate of change for reporters might be interpreted.

$$\frac{dI(t)}{dt} \propto \left(\alpha - I\left(t\right)\right). \tag{4.27}$$

In eqn (4.27), it has been assumed that the rate of change in the number of reporters present at any time point *t* depends on the remaining pool of reporters (which will eventually become the actual reporters of the vulnerability discovered or encountered by thcm). Making use of the hazard rate approach (Bass, 1969), the number of reporters at any time t through eqn (4.27) can be represented as

$$\frac{dI(t)}{dt} = \frac{f(t)}{1 - F(t)} (\alpha - I(t)), \tag{4.28}$$

where $f(t)$ represents the likelihood of vulnerability reporters at time t, and

$$F(t) = \int_0^T f(t)\, dt,\ F(0) = 0. \tag{4.29}$$

Solving eqn (4.28) under the boundary condition $I(t = 0) = 0$, the following expression can be obtained:

$$I(t) = \alpha \cdot F(t). \tag{4.30}$$

It is clear that marketing science contributes a variety of forms to the structure that was produced in eqn (4.30). It is possible to take into consideration various mathematical structures that are presented in published works and talk specifically about the way in which information might move on in the market (Meade & Islam, 1998). This will allow one to capture the vulnerabilities that were revealed by the reporters. For the purpose of modeling, many forms of *F*(*t*) can illustrate multiple patterns in which a piece of information (in this case, the pattern in which a vulnerability can be tracked and reported by the reporter) that can be disseminated in the market is taken into consideration and employed.

Following is a concise explanation of the use of various distributions:

- **Logistic distribution** (Blackman, 1971):
  When it comes to modeling the diffusion pattern, this distribution function is by far the most common one to utilize. It follows an S-shaped pattern of the cumulative number of reporters and describes the spread of information among the reporters. Additionally, the pattern is shaped like an S curve. According to the description of an S-shaped curve, the software system starts to attract users, and those users start reporting flaws. Following the accumulation of adequate knowledge, the total

number of reporters continues to rise throughout the course of time. As more time passes, it continues to rise until the software system reaches the height of its popularity, at which point the reporting rate began to fall and, eventually, reached a level of saturation. After that, it began to level off.

- **Extensions of logistic distribution** (Bass, 1969):
  The literature has a number of different derivations of logistic distributions, among which is the Bass diffusion model, which represents the adoption of a product through both external and internal impacts and which has been taken into consideration here. In this situation, the adoption of information by the reporters has been modeled after the Bass diffusion curve, which may be found in the literature. The curve illustrates a symmetrical behavior and reaches its maximum rate when 50% of its potential reporters are surveyed. When a logistic curve is utilized, this means that the number of reporters at any one time point cannot be more than 50% of the total possible number of reporters.
- **Gompertz distribution** (Harrison & Pearce, 1972):
  The Gompertz distribution is taken into consideration since it provides the model with an increased degree of flexibility, which results in a more accurate forecast. It refers to circumstances in which information regarding a product is disseminated to adopters (reporters) only on the basis of internal influences. In addition, the Gompertz curve is asymmetric and it achieves its maximum growth rate at an earlier stage in comparison to the numerous software products that exhibit an increased popularity after their release period. This is because the Gompertz curve reaches its maximum growth rate at an earlier stage.
- **Normal distribution** (Rogers, 1995); (Stapleton, 1976)
  Normal distribution is used to describe the diffusion process amongst the reporters because of the learning effects of the target system by the reporters. Thus, the number of reporters in the system increases due to the rising popularity of a software and it may influence the remaining pool of reporters. The result of this influence formulates a mathematical function following normal curve over a series of successive periods.
- **Weibull distribution** (Sharif & Islam, 1980):
  Depending on the value of the shape parameter, the Weibull distribution can represent a variety of distinct curves. It did this by shifting both the inflection point and the symmetry. This offered flexibility. It is appropriate for referring to processes that have fluctuating rates, such as those with rising or decreasing rates.

- **Gamma/shifted Gompertz distribution** (Bemmaor, 1992):
  The term "Gompertz distribution" refers to the diverse patterns of behavior exhibited by target users (in this case, reporters) with regard to the likelihood that they are going to accept a product. It considers a constant rate in terms of the likelihood of someone purchasing a thing.

Table 4.1 provides a listing of the utilization functions of all of the patterns that were taken into consideration when modeling the reporters. The distribution function often displays a bell-shaped non-cumulative adoption curve in addition to an S-shaped cumulative adoption curve. This is one of the common characteristics of the function. According to Rogers (1995), the behavior of users (reporters) throughout the course of the time horizon demonstrates a bell-shaped curve. Later on, Mahajan *et al.* investigated the patterns that emerged in the non-cumulative adoption curve (Mahajan et.al., 1990). Their goal was to portray the behavior of adopters in relation to the passage of time. The aforementioned models of diffusion consider a variety of distribution functions, which demonstrate how reporters behave in accordance with symmetric, asymmetric, and flexible patterns, respectively. The number of non-cumulative reports exhibits a growing trend up to its peak due to the popularity of a software product in the market. This philosophy is consistent with what Mahajan *et al.* have mentioned, and it follows the same pattern. And then, as time goes on, there is a gradual decline in sales because customers become less interested in a particular product as a result of the availability of more advanced and competing software.

The discussed components of eqn (4.23) are combined and the proposed model is formulated to capture the effect of available reporters in discovering the vulnerabilities. Substituting eqn (4.26) in eqn (4.23), the following expression can be obtained:

$$\frac{d\Omega(t)}{dt} = \frac{b}{1+\beta \cdot e^{-b \cdot I(t)}} \left(N - \Omega(t)\right) \cdot \frac{dI(t)}{dt}. \tag{4.31}$$

Eqn (4.31) can be further written as

$$\frac{\frac{d\Omega(t)}{dt}}{i(t)} = \frac{b}{1+\beta \cdot e^{-b \cdot I(t)}} \left(N - \Omega(t)\right). \tag{4.32}$$

Solving eqn (4.32) under the initial conditions $\Omega\,(t=0) = 0$ and $I\,(t=0) = 0$, the following expression can be obtained:

$$\Omega\,(t) = N \cdot \left(\frac{1 - e^{-b \cdot I(t)}}{1+\beta \cdot e^{-b \cdot I(t)}}\right). \tag{4.33}$$

Table 4.1 Usage functions under consideration.

Distribution function	Usage function
$F(t)$ ~ Simple logistic distribution	$I_1(t) = \alpha \cdot \left(\frac{1}{1+e^{-\frac{t-\mu}{s}}}\right)$
$F(t)$ ~ Extended logistic distribution	$I_2(t) = \alpha \cdot \left(\frac{1-e^{-(p+q)\cdot t}}{1+\frac{q}{p}\cdot e^{-(p+q)\cdot t}}\right)$
$F(t)$ ~ Gompertz distribution	$I_3(t) = \alpha \cdot \left(1-e^{-\eta(e^{b\cdot t}-1)}\right)$
$F(t)$ ~ Normal distribution	$I_4(t) = \alpha \cdot \int_{-\infty}^{t} \frac{1}{\sqrt{2\pi}\sigma} e^{\left(-\frac{(y-\mu)^2}{2\sigma^2}\right)} dy$
$F(t)$ ~ Weibull distribution	$I_5(t) = \alpha \cdot \left(1-e^{-rt^{\alpha}}\right)$
$F(t)$ ~ Gamma/shifted Gompertz distribution	$I_6(t) = \alpha \cdot \left((1-e^{-b*t}) \cdot e^{-\eta \cdot e^{-b*t}}\right)$

Eqn (4.33) describes the vulnerability discovery with respect to the available reporters in the field. The proposed model is based on the usage function $I(t)$ that describes the behavior of users (reporters) using the software through different distribution functions and is given in Table 4.1. Moreover, the respective $I(t)$ can be used to evaluate the vulnerability discovery phenomenon based on the learning effect of underlying reporters captured by various distribution functions. Hence, the proposed model can be given as

$$\Omega_i(t) = N \cdot \left(\frac{1-e^{-b\cdot I_i(t)}}{1+\beta \cdot e^{-b\cdot I_i(t)}}\right) \qquad i = 1\ldots 6, \tag{4.34}$$

where i stands for the different proposed models denoting different reporters' usage function as described in Table 4.1.

References

Rescorla, E. (2005). Is finding security holes a good idea? *IEEE Security & Privacy, 3*(1), 14-19.

Alhazmi, O. H., & Malaiya, Y. K. (2005b). Quantitative Vulnerability Assessment of Systems Software. *Annual Reliability and Maintainability Symposium* (pp. 615-620). Alexandria, VA, USA: IEEE.

Younis, A. A., Joh, H., & Malaiya, Y. K. (2011). Modeling Learningless Vulnerability Discovery using a Folded Distribution. *International Conference on Security and Management*, (pp. 617-623).

Li, P. L., Shaw, M., Herbsleb, J., Ray, B., & Santhanam, P. (2004, October). Empirical evaluation of defect projection models for widely-deployed production software systems. In Proceedings of the 12th ACM SIGSOFT twelfth international symposium on Foundations of software engineering (pp. 263-272).

Zhou, Y., & Davis, J. (2005). Open source software reliability model: an empirical approach. ACM SIGSOFT software engineering notes, 30(4), 1-6.

Kapur, P. K., Sachdeva, N., & Khatri, S. K. (2015). Vulnerability Discovery Modeling. *International conference on quality, reliability, infocom technology and industrial technology management*, (pp. 34-54). New Delhi.

Lyu, M. R. (1996). *Handbook of Software Reliability Engineering.* USA: McGraw-Hill.

Ozment, A. (2007). Vulnerability Discovery & Software Security. *Ph.D. Dissertation.* Cambridge, UK.: University of Cambridge Computer Laboratory.

Massacci, F., & Nguyen, V. H. (2014). An Empirical Methodology to Evaluate Vulnerability Discovery Models. *IEEE Transactions on Software Engineering, 40*(12), 1147-1162.

Kenny, G. (1993). Estimating defects in commercial software during operational use. *IEEE Transactions on Reliability, 42*(1), 107-115.

Alhazmi, O. H., & Malaiya, Y. K. (2005a). Modeling the vulnerability discovery process. *Proceedings of the 16th IEEE International Symposium on Software Reliability Engineering (ISSRE'05)* (pp. 129-138). Washington, DC, USA: IEEE Computer Society. Retrieved from https://www.cs.colostate.edu/~malaiya/pub/issre05.pdf

Bass, F. (1969). A new product growth for model consumer durables. *Management science, 15*(5), 215-227.

Meade, N., & Islam, T. (1998). Technological Forecasting – Model Selection, Model Stability, and Combining Models. *Management Science, 44*(8), 1115-1130.

Blackman, A. (1971). A mathematical model for trend forecasts. *Technological Forecasting and Social Change, 3*, 441-452.

Harrison, P. J., & Pearce, S. F. (1972). The use of trend curves as an aid to market forecasting. *Industrial Marketing Management, 1*(2), 149-170.

Rogers, E. M. (1995). *Diffusion of Innovation.* New York, USA: The Free Press, Simon and Schuster.

Stapleton, E. (1976). The normal distribution as a model of technological substitution. *Technological Forecasting and Social Change, 8*(3), 325-334.

Sharif, M. N., & Islam, M. N. (1980). The Weibull distribution as a general model for forecasting technological change. *Technological Forecasting and Social Change, 18*(3), 247-256.

Bemmaor, A. C. (1992). Modeling the diffusion of new durable goods: Word-of-mouth effect versus consumer heterogeneity. In G. Laurent, G. L. Lilien, & B. Pras, *Research traditions in marketing* (pp. 201-229). Dordrecht: Springer.

Mahajan, V., Muller, E., & Srivastava, R. K. (1990). Determination of Adopter Categories by Using Innovation Diffusion Models. *Journal of Marketing Research, 27*(1), 37-50.

Kapur, P. K., Pham, H., Gupta, A., & Jha, P. C. (2011). *Software reliability assessment with OR applications* (Vol. 364). London: Springer.

5

Unification-based Modeling

We are cognizant of the fact that today's information society is wholly dependent upon its computer systems. Software systems have not yet reached the level of productivity, quality, and dependability that has been reached by computer hardware systems. These aspects of software are receiving increased attention and focus from software developers and management in recent years, which has led to improvements. In contrast to physical components, all newly developed software must be tested, despite the fact that several methods are utilized throughout the process of developing software in order to fulfill quality criteria for software. The amount of quality that can be obtained via testing is meaningless unless it can be assessed quantitatively in order to instill confidence in the level of dependability that can be attained. In addition to this, several decisions, such as the timing of the release and those pertaining to the allocation of resources and forecasting the post-release patches, may be made with more precision only if a quantitative assessment of quality is available. For all of this, measuring tools are required to evaluate the quality of the software. At this point in time, we are aware that software vulnerability discovery models that are constructed on the basis of stochastic and statistical principles are the essential instruments that have shown to be the most successful in evaluating software trustworthiness quantitatively. Up to now, we have discussed the software vulnerability models based on non-homogeneous Poisson process (NHPP) and most of the VDMs perform differently on different datasets. Thus, in this chapter, we discuss a unified framework that can be utilized in order to identify and model the vulnerabilities discovered in a software.

5.1 Notations

Following are the notations that have been used while modeling the vulnerability discovery process:

$\Omega(t)$: Cumulative number of vulnerabilities discovered by time t.
$f(t)$: Fraction of vulnerabilities discovered at time t.
$F(t)$: Fraction of vulnerabilities discovered by time t.
N: Total number of vulnerabilities present in the software system.
r: Vulnerability discovery rate.
α: Parameter to depict the shape.
β: Parameter to depict learning of detectors.

5.2 Modeling Framework

The vulnerability discovery function is the fundamental component of all of the NHPP models that can be found in the literature. It is a representation of the total number of vulnerabilities that have been found up to the current moment. As a result, the amount of vulnerabilities that are present in the software at any one moment is precisely proportionate to the number of residual vulnerabilities that have not yet been detected. This relationship may be stated as follows:

$$\frac{d\Omega(t)}{dt} \propto (N - \Omega(t)). \tag{5.1}$$

The process of discovering vulnerabilities will detect vulnerabilities at a rate denoted by $r(t)$, and the vulnerabilities that are active at any one moment may be represented mathematically as follows:

$$\frac{d\Omega(t)}{dt} = r(t)(N - \Omega(t)), \tag{5.2}$$

where N is the total number of vulnerabilities that are present in a software system and $r(t)$ is the vulnerability discovery rate that determines how quickly any remaining flaws in software are found. $(N - \Omega(t))$ is the notation used to express the number of unknown vulnerabilities that are still present in a software at time *t*. The count denoted by $(N - \Omega(t))$ is a monotonically non-increasing function of time, since the count $(N - \Omega(t))$ drops as additional vulnerabilities are identified over the course of time. This means that the function does not continue to increase with time. Furthermore, the rate at which the remaining number of vulnerabilities is detected is the primary factor that determines the nature of the total severity of the vulnerability.

It is essential to keep in mind that the severity of the vulnerability is dependent not only on the number of flaws that are still present in a software system, but also on the rate at which the vulnerabilities are identified in comparison to the percentage of the population that is composed of vulnerabilities that have not yet been found. Therefore, the rate at which vulnerabilities are discovered, denoted by the symbol $r(t)$, may be interpreted in terms of the hazard function as follows:

$$\frac{d\Omega(t)}{dt} = \frac{f(t)}{1 - F(t)}(N - \Omega(t)), \tag{5.3}$$

where $f(t)$ is the fraction of vulnerabilities discovered at time t and $F(t)$ is the fraction of vulnerabilities discovered by time t. After solving eqn (5.3) under the initial condition, at time $t = 0$, the number of vulnerabilities discovered is zero, i.e., $\Omega\,(t = 0) = 0$, the cumulative number of vulnerabilities discovered by time t can be obtained as

$$\Omega(t) = N \cdot F(t). \tag{5.4}$$

Therefore, the cumulative number of vulnerabilities that are present in a software system can be identified based on the discovery pattern supplied by any distribution function. These numbers may vary depending on the distribution function. In this section, we discuss some VDMs from a more holistic point of view using the approach that was provided before. These models consider a wide variety of distribution functions, which allows them to accommodate a variety of discovery patterns.

5.2.1 Rescorla exponential model

Due to the fact that it has a constant rate, the exponential distribution is one of the distributions that are utilized the most frequently in the modeling of the anticipated number of flaws or vulnerabilities. It denotes that the process of vulnerability discovery is evenly distributed and that each vulnerability has the same likelihood of being detected during the process of vulnerability discovery. It is anticipated that the finding of software vulnerabilities would follow an exponential distribution in the majority of the software testing efforts. For this reason, an exponential distribution seems appropriate to use throughout the vulnerability finding process.

Using $F(t)$ as exponential distribution to account for the discovery of vulnerability, i.e., assuming:

$$F(t) = \left(1 - e^{-rt}\right), \tag{5.5}$$

where r is the vulnerability discovery rate and the vulnerability discovery rate per remaining number of vulnerabilities is constant and it can be given using the hazard rate approach as

$$r(t) = \frac{f(t)}{1 - F(t)} = \frac{re^{-rt}}{e^{-rt}} = r. \tag{5.6}$$

Here, the vulnerability discovery rate following a constant pattern is also depicted by the model proposed by Rescorla (Rescorla, 2005). Upon substituting eqn (5.5) in eqn (5.4), the following expression can be obtained:

$$\Omega(t) = N\left(1 - e^{-rt}\right). \tag{5.7}$$

The above expression deduced using the hazard rate approach is comparable to the model proposed by Rescorla (2005).

5.2.2 Joha and Malaiya Weibull model

In the case of exponential models, the software system demonstrates a declining vulnerability intensity function during the discovery process. This may be seen as an indication that there is an increase in the level of software protection throughout the course of the vulnerability discovery process. In the vast majority of instances that occur in real life, the degree of vulnerability worsens at first but subsequently improves over the course of time. The Weibull distribution has been shown to be effective in capturing this phenomenon while adopting this behavior of growing and reducing vulnerability intensity due to the value of its shape parameter. This success may be attributed to the fact that the Weibull distribution has been shown to be successful.

If $F(t)$ can be taken as Weibull distribution function to examine the vulnerability discovery process, then

$$F(t) = \left(1 - e^{-rt^{\alpha}}\right), \tag{5.8}$$

where α is the shape parameter that determines the shape of the vulnerability discovery curve and r is the scale parameter that stretches the time duration of vulnerability modeling.

Then, the hazard rate function can be given as

$$r(t) = \frac{f(t)}{1 - F(t)} = \frac{\alpha r t^{\alpha-1} e^{-rt^{\alpha}}}{e^{-rt^{\alpha}}} = \alpha r t^{\alpha-1}. \tag{5.9}$$

Considering the vulnerability discovery rate to follow the pattern given by eqn (5.9), the VDM proposed by Joha and Malaiya can be deduced (Joha

& Malaiya, 2014). Hence, substituting the value of $F(t)$ from eqn (5.8) in eqn (5.4), the following expression can be obtained:

$$\Omega(t) = N\left(1 - e^{-rt^{\alpha}}\right). \tag{5.10}$$

The asymmetric vulnerability discovery rate can be modeled by eqn (5.10) and the model is same as the VDM given by Joha & Malaiya (2014).

5.2.3 Logistic model

It has been noted that the rate of discovering vulnerabilities in the early stage is less efficient in real-life settings due to the fact that detectors become aware of the software. After gaining familiarity with the software, the detector could be able to readily uncover flaws in an exponential form, which would lead to the vulnerability discovery rate having an S-shaped character. Logistic distribution has the potential to reflect this quality of the vulnerability detection process, which is necessary for the assertion of this perspective.

If the vulnerability discovery is based on the logistic pattern, then the cumulative distribution function for the vulnerabilities can be taken as logistic distribution as

$$F(t) = 1 - \frac{(1+\beta)e^{-rt}}{1+\beta e^{-rt}}, \tag{5.11}$$

where r represents the vulnerability discovery rate and β signifies the parameter that captures the learning phenomenon and also describes the extent of S-shaped nature. Then, the hazard rate function can be given as

$$r(t) = \frac{f(t)}{1 - F(t)} = \frac{r}{1+\beta e^{-rt}}. \tag{5.12}$$

The above vulnerability discovery rate function signifies the discovery of vulnerabilities in logistic pattern. Upon solving the differential equation given in eqn (5.2) and by making use of vulnerability discovery rate pattern as given in eqn (5.12), the model proposed by Kapur et al. (2015) can be obtained (Kapur et al., 2015). Hence, using the hazard rate approach, on substituting the value of $F(t)$ from eqn (5.11) in eqn (5.4), the following expression can be obtained:

$$\Omega(t) = N\left(\frac{1 - e^{-rt}}{1+\beta e^{-rt}}\right). \tag{5.13}$$

The model proposed using the hazard rate approach is comparable to the model proposed by Kapur et al. (2015).

5.2.4 Anand and Bhatt's hump-shaped model

The scenario of the vulnerability discovery phenomena may be examined further while taking the vulnerability discovery rate or the hazard rate to follow a specific pattern signified by a hump-shaped curve. This will allow for a more accurate representation of the situation. The desirability of software shifts over the course of time, which results in varying rates at which vulnerabilities are found and exploited by malicious actors. To be more explicit, once the software product is made available on the market, the majority of the detectors are impacted by the attractiveness of the software. Because more and more people are aware of it and make use of it, each new release has the potential to attract a growing number of users in the early phase. This, in turn, will raise the pace at which vulnerabilities are discovered. After the maximum number of detectors has been reached, that number will begin to fall because, as time passes, the software will become less appealing to users, and fewer individuals will be interested in locating the vulnerability. Utilizing the first derivative of the logistic function allows one to forecast the rising and falling trend of the vulnerability finding rate.

If $F\,(t)$ can be considered as

$$F(t) = \left(1 - e^{\left(-r\left\{\left(\frac{1}{1+\beta e^{-rt}}\right)-\left(\frac{1}{1+\beta}\right)\right\}\right)}\right), \tag{5.14}$$

where r is the parameter depicting the rate by which vulnerabilities are discovered and β denotes the learning parameter describing the S-shaped of the curve, then the hazard rate function can be given as

$$r(t) = \frac{f(t)}{1-F(t)} = \frac{r^2\beta e^{-rt}}{(1+\beta e^{-rt})^2}. \tag{5.15}$$

On substituting the value of $F(t)$ from eqn (5.14) in eqn (5.4), the cumulative number of vulnerabilities discovered can be modeled as

$$\Omega(t) = N\left(1 - e^{-r\left\{\left(\frac{1}{1+\beta e^{-rt})-\left(\frac{1}{1+\beta}\right)}\right)\right.}\right). \tag{5.16}$$

Eqn (5.16) is the same as the VDM formulated by Anand & Bhatt (2016).

References

Rescorla, E. (2005). Is finding security holes a good idea? *IEEE Security & Privacy, 3*(1), 14-19.

Joha, H., & Malaiya, Y. K. (2014). Modeling Skewness in Vulnerability Discovery. *Quality & Reliability Engineering International, 30*(8), 1445-1459.

Kapur, P. K., Sachdeva, N., & Khatri, S. K. (2015). Vulnerability Discovery Modeling. *International conference on quality, reliability, infocom technology and industrial technology management*, (pp. 34-54). New Delhi.

Anand, A., & Bhatt, N. (2016). Vulnerability discovery modeling and weighted criteria based ranking. Journal of the Indian Society for Probability and Statistics, 17, 1-10.

6

Characterizing and Categorizing Software Vulnerabilities

In spite of the advancements achieved in computer programming and the associated practices of software engineering, nearly all of the software that are utilized in day-to-day life still contain a significant number of errors. However, after the software has been made available to the public, some of the bugs that are discovered are undeniably more dangerous than others. When a vulnerability is found, members of the security community may classify it as belonging to a given category depending on the different ways in which it might affect a software system. The behavior of the vulnerability is the sole factor used to determine this allocation. The focus of the investigation is on determining how many flaws may be found in a software through the use of quantitative analysis. As discussed in Chapter 1, the vulnerability detection process has been found to be a dependent process. To put it another way, the process of identifying vulnerabilities might result in the identification of some previously unknown vulnerabilities. The dependence on the discovery of vulnerabilities may be caused by a number of factors, including the following: finding a vulnerability in a software product that shares its code with another product; discovering new vulnerabilities while investigating previously discovered vulnerabilities; or discovering a vulnerability as a result of the influence of vulnerabilities of other types. Despite this, the procedure for discovering vulnerabilities is always evolving as time goes on. Examining the trend in both the noncumulative discovery function and its rate of change may assist determine how a certain proportion of vulnerabilities are found in each period. This can be done by gaining an understanding of the rate at which the discovery rate is changing. Furthermore, it is essential to analyze how the discovery pattern impacts in the discovery of vulnerabilities each time it contributes a change in the rate of discovery. This is because the discovery pattern affects the pace at which vulnerabilities are discovered.

In this chapter, we discuss how the VDM can be used to characterize the vulnerabilities based on the identification of additional vulnerabilities. In the first section of the chapter, we discuss a mathematical framework that can be used to quantify the vulnerabilities that have been found and evaluate those vulnerabilities depending on the effect of any other vulnerabilities that have been found. The second part offers a concise summary of vulnerabilities by investigating the patterns and the influence of the learning phenomena in the process of classifying the vulnerabilities according to the period at which they were discovered.

6.1 Independence of Vulnerability Discovery

One of the important assumptions of VDM is that the vulnerability discoveries occur independently. On the other hand, there is some evidence to suggest that they do not. The NVD data on vulnerabilities are taken into consideration by Gopalakrishna and Spaford. They classified these vulnerabilities utilizing both the NVD and Aslam *et al.* classification schemes (Aslam et al., 1996). It is interesting to note that they discovered that "two successive vulnerabilities are considered in a software product, and in one-third of those cases, they are of the same type." This finding led them to think that vulnerability detection is not independent, despite the fact that input validation mistakes make up half of the vulnerabilities and may have biased the results in a certain direction. They next carry out a run test in order to verify whether or not the data are independent, and they get contradictory results: for each unique product, the finding of vulnerabilities in certain categories is dependent, while in others it is independent (Gopalakrishna & Spafford, 2005). Given these findings, it is clear that any modeling attempt should begin by determining whether or not the vulnerability data can be considered independent.

If vulnerability data is dependent, it may be because vulnerability hunters are searching for more instances of the same sort of vulnerability that has recently been identified – and developers may make the same kind of error more than once. For instance, a programmer might constantly insert a duplicate of size LENGTH into a buffer, even when the size of the buffer is really one byte less than LENGTH. Detectors receive benefits as a result of their efforts to hunt for further or comparable examples of the same kind of vulnerability. In the same manner, additional problems that are not connected to security might be created. On the other hand, SRGMs are often applied to failure data received during automated testing. As a consequence of this, the finding of these defects is carried out independently.

On the other hand, it is feasible that VDMs can be applied to vulnerability detection events. A vulnerability detection event is an independent act of detection that can lead to the identification of many instances of dependent vulnerabilities. The preceding paragraph provided a description of a fictitious program that consistently and incorrectly carried out a copy operation with the size LENGTH. In the above scenario, the introduction of a vulnerability occurs each time that copy operation is carried out in the source code; nevertheless, the identification of all of these individual vulnerabilities may be consolidated into a single detection event.

A common presumption behind vulnerability discovery methods is that the data to which they are applied reflects a series of independent occurrences. Regrettably, the discovery of vulnerabilities is typically a dependent process. In this chapter, we discuss this important framework and introduce a methodical framework that captures this phenomenon.

6.2 Reasons for Dependence of Detection

Here we outline some reasons that could result in the reasons for detection dependence as outlined by Ozment (Ozment, 2007). The discovery of a new kind of vulnerability, a place that had not been investigated before, and a new instrument for identifying vulnerabilities are the three basic reasons for dependency in the detection of vulnerabilities. Each of these factors can lead to the rapid identification of a significant number of vulnerabilities of the same type within a short period of time.

It has been observed that a single conceptual error may often be the cause of the discovery of other vulnerabilities. This is the case in many different situations. In May 2004, for instance, it was announced that the OpenBSD operating system included a vulnerability (Esser, 2004a). As a result of the examination of the vulnerability, six other vulnerabilities in the same program were found (Esser, 2004b). In addition to this, it has been discovered that a single vulnerability in Microsoft Windows 7 has the potential to activate many distinct sorts of vulnerabilities that are present in a software application. A single defect in the OLE Automation system and VBScript scripting engine can result in four distinct vulnerabilities, such as denial of service, execution of arbitrary code, overflow, and memory corruption. This is similar to the situation described in a CVE entry CVE-2016-3375.

Another factor that contributes to dependency is the development of a tool that makes it possible for scanners to identify vulnerabilities. These kinds of technologies have the potential to lead to the discovery of vulnerabilities of a wide variety, located in a variety of spots throughout a single program or across many programs. It is quite likely that the execution of such a tool will lead to a cluster of vulnerabilities, which may then violate the independence assumption established by VDMs. For instance, in 2002, academics from the University of Oulu built the Protos SNMPv1 test suite. This is an example of a "fuzzer," which is a type of program that creates sample inputs to other programs in an effort to determine the precise inputs that result in program failure. At least four separate vulnerabilities of at least two distinct categories were discovered by this program. In addition, these security flaws were present in a broad number of other programs, all of which were able to implement the SNMPv1 protocol.

6.3 Modeling and Characterizing Vulnerabilities

The models for discovering vulnerabilities assume that the vulnerability intensity, or the quantity of vulnerabilities identified at any given time point, is proportional to the number of vulnerabilities that have not yet been detected. On the other hand, it has been observed that a single conceptual fault may often be the cause of the identification of further vulnerabilities. This is the case in many different cases. As a result, the discovery of a single vulnerability during the process of finding vulnerabilities might be the catalyst for the discovery of more vulnerabilities. To mathematically describe the situation, the following notations are used:

$\Omega(t)$: Cumulative number of vulnerabilities discovered by time t.
N : Total number of vulnerabilities present in the software system.
r : Coefficient describing the rate by which vulnerability is discovered.
s : Coefficient describing the rate by which additional vulnerabilities are discovered.

When a piece of software is made available to consumers, researchers often unearth previously unknown security flaws. While the vulnerabilities are being identified, some other vulnerabilities are discovered as a result of the many factors that have already been described. Because of this, the rate of change in the number of vulnerabilities may be considered to be controlled by two different factors: the pace at which any existing undiscovered flaws are found, as well as the rate at which any fresh vulnerabilities are found. The following differential equation was employed in order to provide a mathematical representation of the situation described above:

$$\frac{d\Omega(t)}{dt} = r\left(N - \Omega(t)\right) + s\frac{\Omega(t)}{N}\left(N - \Omega(t)\right). \tag{6.1}$$

In eqn (6.1), the first component corresponds to the rate by which unique vulnerabilities are discovered and the second factor represents additional vulnerabilities that are detected due to the influence of vulnerabilities that are discovered by time t.

Solving eqn (6.1) with the initial condition $\Omega\,(t = 0) = 0$, the expression for cumulative number of vulnerabilities discovered by time t can be obtained as

$$\Omega\,(t) = N\left(\frac{1 - e^{-(r+s)t}}{1 + \frac{s}{r}e^{-(r+s)t}}\right). \tag{6.2}$$

The nature of the model is such that it is adaptable; the parameters *s* and *r* have the ability to define the form of the discovery curve. It is able to represent the discovery curve as having both an exponential and an S-shaped pattern. If *s* is equal to zero, then eqn (6.2) may be simplified into an exponential model (Rescorla, 2005). In addition, the finding phenomena can be characterized by a development curve in the shape of an S, as Alhazmi and Malaiya have proposed (Alhazmi & Malaiya, 2005a). The significance of the value of (s/r) determines the form that the S-shaped discovery curve takes. This behavior of the VDM may be explained by the learning process that the detector experiences about the software system. In the software reliability studies, it is noteworthy to notice that the behavior of the given model can be equivalent to the model that Kapur and Garg developed (Kapur & Garg, 1992).

6.3.1 Characterizing the vulnerabilities

It is possible to acquire more useful information by analytically analyzing the suggested model and making use of the analogy presented in Mahajan et al. (1990). For instance, the period of time during which the rate of vulnerability detection is at its highest may be determined. The one-of-a-kind structure of a vulnerability identification process is characterized by the differential equation that is presented in eqn (6.1). It is also possible to write it as

$$\frac{dF(t)}{dt} = r\,(1 - F(t)) + (sF(t))\,(1 - F(t))\,, \tag{6.3}$$

where $F\,(t)$ represents the distribution pattern describing the pattern in which vulnerabilities are discovered. Upon solving eqn (6.3), it yields an S-shaped cumulative distribution function that can be described as

$$F\,(t) = \left(\frac{1 - e^{-(r+s)t}}{1 + \frac{s}{r}e^{-(r+s)t}}\right). \tag{6.4}$$

Further, differentiating eqn (6.4) can provide the noncumulative distribution pattern for the vulnerability discovery and is given by

$$f(t) = \frac{r(r+s)^2 e^{-(r+s)t}}{\left(r + se^{-(r+s)t}\right)^2}. \tag{6.5}$$

In eqn (6.3), the term $r\,(1 - F(t))$ refers to the proportion of unique vulnerabilities detected by the detector that are not discovered owing to the influence of existing vulnerabilities discovered. Second, the term $sF(t)\,(1 - F(t))$ denotes the fraction of vulnerabilities that are affected as a result of the identification of vulnerabilities that were reported in the past. As a result, the percentage of vulnerabilities found throughout the process of discovery may be visualized in Figure 6.1. The vulnerabilities that are brought about by the first element may be referred to as leading or primary vulnerabilities, whereas the flaws that are brought about by the second factor can be referred to as additional or supplementary vulnerabilities.

Moreover, to capture the proportion of discovered vulnerabilities due to the above stated two factors a mathematical analysis is presented. The $F(t)$ denotes the cumulative distribution by which the vulnerabilities are discovered by time t. As considered in the model, $F(t)$ inhibits two components, *viz.*, $F_1(t)$ the proportion representing the unique vulnerabilities that are discovered without any influence and $F_2(t)$ corresponds to the proportion

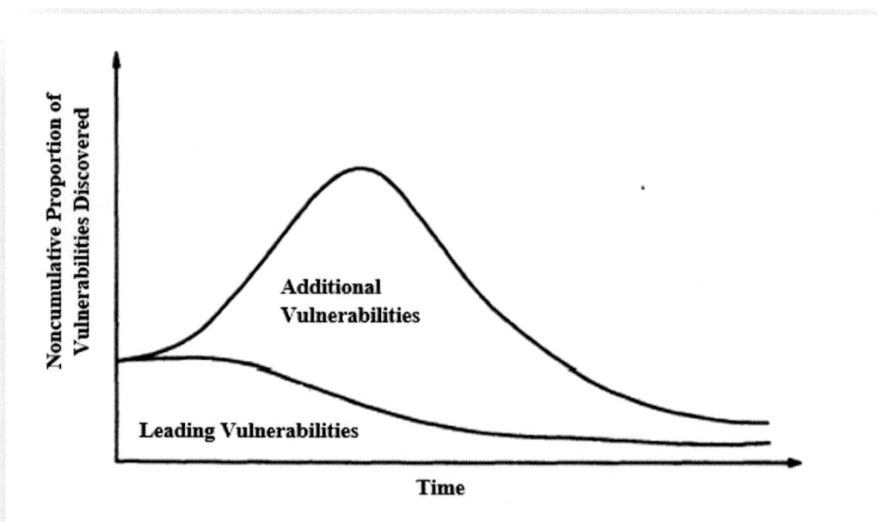

Figure 6.1 Leading and additional vulnerabilities (Source: Bhatt *et al.*, 2017).

of vulnerabilities that are additionally discovered due to the influence of previously discovered vulnerabilities. Thus, $r\,(1 - F(t))$ gives the fraction of vulnerabilities reported uniquely at time t. Hence, the total fraction of discovery of unique vulnerabilities, $F_1(t)$, between any two time periods, say t_0 and t_F, can be given as

$$F_1\,(t) = r \int_{t_0}^{t_F} (1 - F(t))\,dt. \tag{6.6}$$

Because $F(t)$ is given in eqn (6.4), eqn (6.6) can be rewritten as

$$F_1\,(t) = r \int_{t_0}^{t_F} \left(1 - \frac{1 - e^{-(r+s)t}}{1 + \frac{s}{r}e^{-(r+s)t}}\right) dt. \tag{6.7}$$

This gives after integrating,

$$F_1\,(t) = \frac{r}{s} ln \left(\frac{r + se^{-(r+s)t_0}}{r + se^{-(r+s)t_F}}\right). \tag{6.8}$$

Substitution of $t_0 = 0$ and $t_F = t$ in eqn (6.8) yields

$$F_1\,(t) = \frac{r}{s}\left(\frac{1 + \frac{r}{s}}{1 + \frac{r}{s}e^{-(r+s)t}}\right). \tag{6.9}$$

Eqn (6.9) denotes the cumulative proportion of vulnerabilities that are uniquely discovered or are not influenced by other vulnerabilities and, hence, the cumulative proportion of additional vulnerabilities discovered due to the influence of previously discovered vulnerabilities can be given by $F_2\,(t) = 1 - F_1(t)$, that is,

$$F_2\,(t) = \left(1 - \frac{r}{s}\left(\frac{1 + \frac{r}{s}}{1 + \frac{r}{s}e^{-(r+s)t}}\right)\right). \tag{6.10}$$

On multiplying eqn (6.9) and (6.10) with N provides the cumulative vulnerabilities discovery curve segmenting the number of vulnerabilities discovered for each case over the period of time.

6.3.1.1 Empirical evaluation

The NLLS approach has been taken into consideration for the purpose of evaluating the parameters, and the model has been assessed using data from CVEDetails on four distinct vulnerability datasets, namely Windows XP,

Windows Server 2008, Mac OS X, and Mac OS X Server (Windows Xp, 2016); (Mac Os X Server, 2016); (Mac Os X, 2016); (Windows Server 2008, 2016). The data for these evaluations was gathered. In light of the fact that the suggested model predicts that the discovery phenomena would follow an S-shaped curve, it is then contrasted with the AML model, which similarly represents nature in an S-shaped pattern. Table 6.1 presents the parameter estimates for both of the models that were considered.

Table 6.1 Model parameter estimation results.

Parameter estimates	Windows XP	Windows Server 2008	Apple Mac OS X	Apple Mac OS X Server
	Eqn (6.2)	Eqn (6.2)	Eqn (6.2)	Eqn (6.2)
N	942.15	566.13	1599.72	654.85
r	0.0107	0.0217	0.0118	0.0134
s	0.3059	0.6612	0.2338	0.5254
c	–	–	–	–

In contrast to the dataset used, the best values of the criterion are provided by Apple Mac OS X Server. Moreover, the value of parameter (s/r) provides the S-shaped character of the fitted model to the dataset. It has been found that the value of (s/r) of the model represented by eqn (6.2) is the highest for the dataset Apple Mac OS X Server. The extent of S-shaped nature can be attributed by the value of (s/r).

Further, Tables 6.2 and 6.3 present the cumulative number of observed and predicted vulnerabilities along with the proportion of leading vulnerabilities discovered and additional vulnerabilities discovered due to the previously discovered vulnerabilities.

The discovery phenomena for leading vulnerabilities in Windows XP and Apple Mac OS X software are shown in Tables 6.2 and 6.3, which can be noticed above. This phenomenon shows that a significant portion of leading vulnerabilities contributes to the discovery process. After a specific amount of time has passed, the discovery process is affected by the identification of more vulnerabilities. It is possible that this is because of a learning phenomenon that occurs within the detectors, which means that they understand the software system and are aware of the many kinds of vulnerabilities that are likely to be found. On the other hand, the proportion of additional vulnerabilities has a bigger role in the discovery process for software running Windows Server 2008 and Mac OS X Server. Due to the fact that these software products share

Table 6.2 Bifurcation of vulnerabilities for Microsoft Windows products.

	Windows XP				Windows Server 2008				
Time	Observed	Predicted	Leading vulnerabilities	Additional vulnerabilities	Time	Observed	Predicted	Leading vulnerabilities	Additional vulnerabilities
1	1	12	10	2	1	1	17	12	5
2	11	27	20	7	2	21	48	24	24
3	45	48	30	18	3	99	100	34	66
4	67	75	39	36	4	190	177	44	134
5	111	110	48	61	5	295	274	51	222
6	177	153	57	96	6	346	370	56	313
7	233	205	65	140	7	450	447	60	387
8	267	266	73	193	8	488	499	62	437
9	301	336	80	256	9	543	530	63	467
10	389	411	86	325	–	–	–	–	–
11	487	488	91	396	–	–	–	–	–
12	588	563	96	467	–	–	–	–	–
13	632	634	100	534	–	–	–	–	–
14	720	696	102	594	–	–	–	–	–
15	727	750	105	645	–	–	–	–	–

their source code with their predecessors, any vulnerabilities that were found in the products that came before them also affected them.

6.3.2 Categorization of vulnerabilities

There are a few different VDMs that can be found in the published research that classify the discovery process based on the detector, the attractiveness of the software, and the related discovery pattern. On the other hand, these models may be used to determine the rate of vulnerability discovery at any given moment in time. On the other hand, a comprehensive mathematical depiction of the vulnerability characterization was covered in the previous section. This was done so that the vulnerabilities could be characterized according to the pattern in which they were discovered. In this part, some

Table 6.3 Bifurcation of vulnerabilities for Apple products.

	Apple Mac OS X				Apple Mac OS X Server				
Time	Observed	Predicted	Leading vulnerabilities	Additional vulnerabilities	Time	Observed	Predicted	Leading vulnerabilities	Additional vulnerabilities
1	1	21	19	2	1	2	11	9	3
2	6	47	37	10	2	16	30	17	13
3	26	80	55	24	3	58	60	26	35
4	51	119	73	46	4	130	105	33	72
5	105	167	90	76	5	185	168	40	128
6	201	223	107	116	6	238	248	46	202
7	307	289	123	166	7	321	337	51	286
8	413	365	138	227	8	404	424	55	369
9	506	450	152	298	9	508	498	57	440
10	587	543	165	377	10	575	553	59	494
11	684	642	177	465	11	606	592	60	531
12	756	744	188	556	12	615	616	61	556
13	791	847	197	650	13	626	632	61	571
14	854	947	206	742	14	627	641	62	580
15	968	1042	213	830	–	–	–	–	–
16	1249	1130	219	911	–	–	–	–	–

more analysis is discussed by means of a mathematical study of the trends in the instantaneous discovery rate.

6.3.2.1 Time point analysis

Here we discuss a further investigation of the vulnerability discovery process and classify the vulnerabilities into different heads based on their time of discovery. It can be done by analyzing the trend in both the instantaneous vulnerability discovery rate $\Omega'(t)$ and its rate of change $\frac{d\Omega'(t)}{dt} = \Omega''(t)$. It is possible to calculate the noncumulative instantaneous vulnerability discovery rate at any given instant *t* by calculating the first derivative of eqn (6.2), from which one can derive the rate of change in vulnerability discovery using the following formula:

$$\Omega'(t) = \frac{d\Omega(t)}{dt} = N\left(\frac{r(r+s)^2 e^{-(r+s)t}}{\left(r + se^{-(r+s)t}\right)^2}\right). \tag{6.11}$$

The time at which the vulnerability discovery rate is maximum can be found by equating eqn (6.10) to zero, and is given as

$$T^* = -\frac{1}{(r+s)}\ln\left(\frac{r}{s}\right). \quad (6.12)$$

The noncumulative vulnerability discovery curve can be visualized as given in Figure 6.2 and suggests the occurrence of times T_1 and T_2 that indicate a shift in the instantaneous vulnerability discovery rate. These times signify the change in the rate at which vulnerabilities are discovered. At each of the inflection points, the form of the noncumulative vulnerability discovery curve undergoes a change. As a result of the fact that the cumulative vulnerability finding curve seems to be in the shape of an S, whereas the noncumulative vulnerability discovery curve looks more like a bell-shaped curve that has two inflection points in it. Therefore, the same line of reasoning may be utilized analytically in order to build the vulnerability classification based on the suggested VDM. It is possible to compute T_1 and T_2, which stand for the inflection points of $\Omega'(t)$, using the appropriate mathematics.

In the past, the vulnerabilities were classified based on a variety of parameters, such as the severity of the vulnerability, the types of vulnerabilities, and so on. Here we discuss an alternative approach in which the vulnerabilities are located according to the times of occurrence. During the discovery phase, it is standard practice to look for vulnerabilities in pathways or places that are more often conducted in the operational environment. This is done rather than searching for vulnerabilities in paths that are traveled when unusual or infrequent conditions are present. In addition, as was said in the preceding section, the discovery of some vulnerabilities might potentially affect the

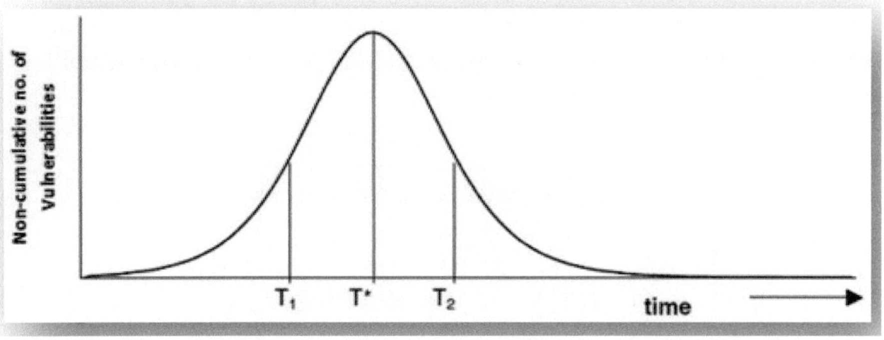

Figure 6.2 Noncumulative vulnerability discovery curve (Bhatt et al., 2018).

identification of other vulnerabilities. Nevertheless, the shift in the immediate vulnerability discovery rate is the cause of this one-of-a-kind trend of finding vulnerabilities. After the introduction of a software product, individuals started to learn about the product, which resulted in the identification of fewer vulnerabilities, as suggested by Alhazmi & Malaiya (2005a). The process of vulnerability detection is often kicked off by the internal detectors due to the fact that the external detectors are still gathering information about the product during the beginning phase. After gaining a comprehension of the software, a number of detectors start identifying vulnerabilities by looking for problematic code in the portions of the software that are run the most frequently. The investigation of previously found vulnerabilities can also impact the finding of further vulnerabilities that may be discovered at a later time.

The trends in the instantaneous vulnerability discovery rate imply that there may be variations in the discovery pattern that the detectors may display in the process of detecting the vulnerabilities over the course of the time period. Table 6.4 provides a concise summary of the trend for the VDM considered in this chapter, which is given in eqn (6.2).

It has been observed in the real-life cases that a large number of vulnerabilities can be discovered during the initial stage of the discovery process. Accordingly, the trend observed in the instantaneous discovery rate increases can be discussed in various time intervals as follows:

- In the interval $(0, T^*)$, the instantaneous discovery rate increases with an increasing rate. It can be attributed due to various reasons such as change in usage environment, availability of a software that shares its code, attractiveness of a software, etc., which suggest an increasing discovery rate at the beginning of the discovery process.
- Once time T_1 has been reached, the discovery process begins to gradually advance at a rate that is gradually diminishing. The vulnerabilities that were identified within the time period (T_1, T^*) have a considerable

Table 6.4 Trend in the instantaneous vulnerability discovery rate.

Time interval	Trend in $\Omega'(t)$
Zero to T_1	Increasing at an increasing rate
T_1 to T^*	Increasing at a decreasing rate
T^* to T_2	Decreasing at an increasing rate
Beyond T_2	Decreasing at a decreasing rate

influence from the vulnerabilities that were discovered in the past. During this interval, the software is presumed to have been adopted by a large number of users, and as a result, the vulnerabilities reported from external sources will have an impact on the discovery process. This is because the detectors will understand the product and discover those vulnerabilities that are likely to appear in software or are related to vulnerabilities that have been discovered in the past.

- The point T^* is the inflection point for the cumulative vulnerability discovery curve, which is denoted by $\Omega(t)$, and it is analogous to the point of maximum for the noncumulative vulnerability discovery rate, denoted by the $\Omega'(t)$. The immediate vulnerability discovery rate falls, which may be linked to the indifference displayed by users when the software system started to be replaced by newer versions. The vulnerability discovery rate declines during the interval (T^*, T_2), which means that the instantaneous vulnerability discovery rate lowers. The decrease in the discovery rate may be ascribed, in part, to the release of a competing software package that has a greater number of features. It is possible that within this time period, the software companies will internally issue an updated version of their product. And the majority of vulnerabilities that are discovered during this time interval are due to vulnerabilities that are discovered in the successive version of the software that shares its code.
- In the interval (T_2, ∞), the vulnerability discovery rate decreases with decreasing rate and the noncumulative curve becomes asymptotic to the time axis. The vulnerabilities accounting in this interval are those that are harder to locate or are afterlife vulnerabilities because these many vulnerabilities would be discovered after the software's end-of-life.

To identify the count of vulnerabilities to be discovered in each time interval for developing the vulnerability categories, a respective count of vulnerabilities underlying in each category based on the discussed time interval can be computed. That is, the number of vulnerabilities to be discovered in each time intervals. For this purpose, it is required to calculate the time points T_1 and T_2. The point of inflection or the transition points T_1 and T_2 can be found by taking a derivative of $\Omega'(t)$.

As described by eqn (6.4), the cumulative distribution function for the vulnerability discovery function can be given as

$$F(t) = \left(\frac{1 - e^{-(r+s)t}}{1 + \frac{s}{r} \cdot e^{-(r+s)t}} \right). \tag{6.13}$$

Further, differentiating eqn (6.13) can provide the noncumulative discovery pattern for the vulnerability discovery and is given by

$$f\left(t\right)=\frac{r(r+s)^2e^{-(r+s)t}}{\left(r+s\cdot e^{-(r+s)t}\right)^2}. \tag{6.14}$$

To find the maximum value of the noncumulative discovery function given in eqn (6.14), its derivative can be obtained and upon equating it to zero, the time at which the noncumulative is maximum can be obtained as

$$\frac{df\left(t\right)}{dt}=\frac{-r(r+s)^3e^{-(r+s)t}}{\left(r+s{\cdot}e^{-(r+s)t}\right)^3}\left(r-s\cdot e^{-(r+s)t}\right)=0, \tag{6.15}$$

$$r-s\cdot e^{-(r+s)t}=0, \tag{6.16}$$

$$T^*=-\frac{1}{(r+s)}\ln\left(\frac{r}{s}\right). \tag{6.17}$$

To find the inflection points of the function given in eqn (6.14), the second derivative of eqn (6.14) can be calculated and is given as

$$\begin{aligned}\frac{d^2f(t)}{dt^2}=&\frac{-r(r+s)^4e^{-(r+s)t}}{\left(r+s{\cdot}e^{-(r+s)t}\right)^4}\left(r+s\cdot e^{-(r+s)t}\right)\left(-r+2s\cdot e^{-(r+s)t}\right),\\&+3s\cdot e^{-(r+s)t}\left(r-s\cdot e^{-(r+s)t}\right).\end{aligned} \tag{6.18}$$

Equating eqn (6.18) to zero, the following expression can be obtained:

$$\left(r+s\cdot e^{-(r+s)t}\right)\left(-r+2s\cdot e^{-(r+s)t}\right)+3s\cdot e^{-(r+s)t}\left(r-s\cdot e^{-(r+s)t}\right)=0. \tag{6.19}$$

Let $Z=e^{-(r+s)t}$; then eqn (6.19) can be written as

$$\left(r+s\cdot Z\right)\left(2s\cdot Z-r\right)+3s\cdot Z\left(r-s\cdot Z\right)=0. \tag{6.20}$$

On simplifying eqn (6.20), a quadratic equation in Z can be obtained as

$$s^2Z^2-4rsZ+r^2=0. \tag{6.21}$$

Therefore,

$$Z=e^{-(r+s)t}=\frac{4rs\pm\sqrt{16r^2s^2-4r^2s^2}}{2s^2}=\frac{r}{s}\left(2\pm\sqrt{3}\right), \tag{6.22}$$

or

$$t = -\frac{1}{(r+s)}\ln\left(\left(2 \pm \sqrt{3}\right)\frac{r}{s}\right). \tag{6.23}$$

The expression for T_1 and T_2 can be given as

$$T_1 = -\frac{1}{(r+s)}\ln\left(\left(2 + \sqrt{3}\right)\frac{r}{s}\right), \tag{6.24}$$

$$T_2 = -\frac{1}{(r+s)}\ln\left(\left(\frac{1}{(2 + \sqrt{3})}\right)\frac{r}{s}\right). \tag{6.25}$$

Using T_1 and T_2, the number of vulnerabilities of each category present in the software can be computed.

6.3.2.2 Vulnerability categories

The first category consists of those numbers of vulnerabilities that are discovered when the instantaneous discovery rate suggests an increasing rate and can be given as

$$V_1 = \Omega(T_1) = N \cdot \left(\frac{1}{3+\sqrt{3}} - \frac{2+\sqrt{3}}{3+\sqrt{3}} \cdot \frac{r}{s}\right) - r \cdot N. \tag{6.26}$$

After a piece of software is made available to the public, a certain number of flaws in it will be found to exist, and the instantaneous vulnerability discovery rate will, as a result of the desirability of the product, create an ever-increasing trend. In addition, the vulnerabilities that have been found will contain a significant number of instances of specific sorts of vulnerabilities that are simple to identify.

Because of the effect of the installed base, the majority of vulnerabilities that are found during the identification process for the second category will be located. The vulnerabilities that were found account for a sizeable fraction of the problems that were reported by consumers. Calculating the total number of vulnerabilities that fall under this category may be done as follows:

$$V_2 = \Omega(T^*) - \Omega(T_1) = \frac{N}{2\sqrt{3}}\left(1 + \frac{r}{s}\right). \tag{6.27}$$

After the software reaches the peak of its popularity, at time point T^*, the vulnerability discovery rate starts to decrease. The vulnerabilities are reported or discovered in a decreasing fashion, and by the time it reaches the time point T_2, the saturation phase starts. An equal number of vulnerabilities are likely to be discovered during the interval (T_1, T^*) due to the symmetricity of the curve. The vulnerabilities constituted during this time interval are mainly due to availability of the new version that shares its code with its previous version. The count of vulnerabilities captured in the interval (T^*, T_2) can be given as

$$V_3 = \Omega(T_2) - \Omega(T^*) = \frac{N}{2\sqrt{3}}\left(1 + \frac{r}{s}\right). \tag{6.28}$$

The instantaneous vulnerability discovery rate finally begins to slow down, or the cumulative number of vulnerabilities begins to asymptotically approach its maximum value. Due to the fact that the software has reached the end of its lifecycle, the vulnerabilities that were found during this period are substantially more difficult to find than the afterlife vulnerabilities. In addition, the vulnerabilities that were found during this time period would be exploitable by a specific number of users who have not upgraded to a more recent version of the software. The count of potential vulnerabilities that extends beyond the time point T_2 is calculated as

$$V_4 = N - \Omega(T_2) = \frac{N}{3+\sqrt{3}}\left(1 + \frac{r}{s}\right). \tag{6.29}$$

6.3.3 Empirical evaluation

This section deals with the empirical results deduced using the proposed methodology for the vulnerability categorization. Here, VDM discussed in Section 6.1 has been considered and then the desired inflection points for the determination of number of vulnerabilities in each category have been calculated. Table 6.5 lists out the parameter estimates for the four datasets used earlier. The noncumulative curves are presented in Figures 6.3– 6.6 for all the four vulnerability datasets. And, the inflection points of the noncumulative curves are calculated and given in Table 6.6.

Table 6.5 Model parameter estimation results.

Parameter estimates	Dataset			
	Windows XP	Windows Server 2008	Apple Mac OS X	Apple Mac OS X Server
N	942.15	566.13	1599.72	654.85
r	0.0107	0.0217	0.0118	0.0134
s	0.3059	0.6612	0.2338	0.5254

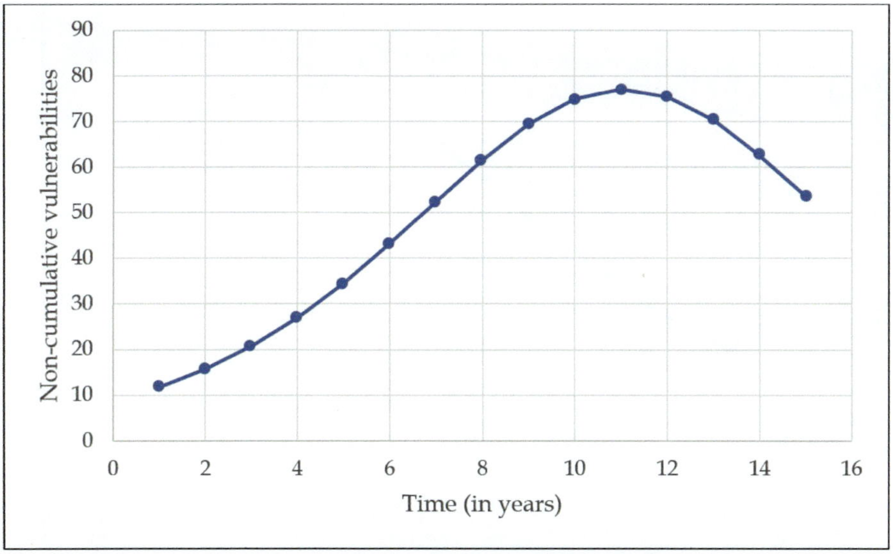

Figure 6.3 Noncumulative curve (Windows XP) (Source: Bhatt et al., 2018).

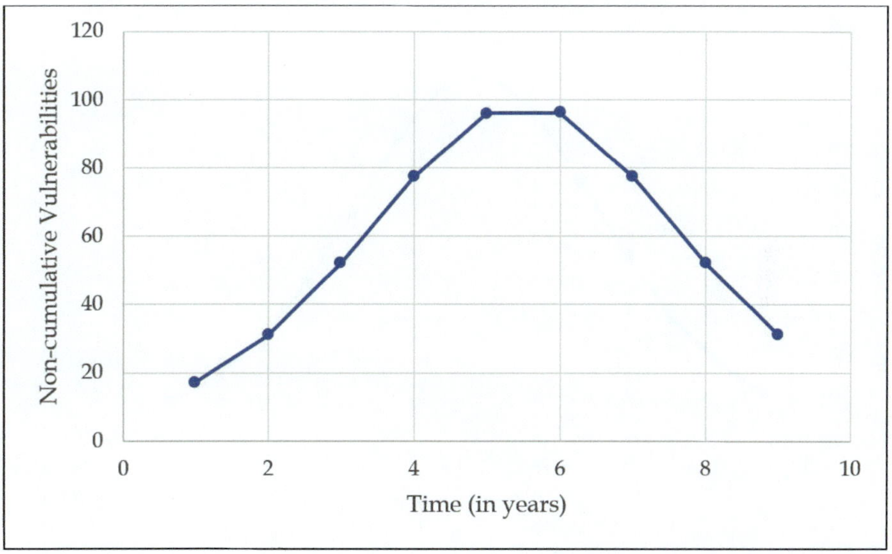

Figure 6.4 Noncumulative curve (Windows Server 2008) (Source: Bhatt et al., 2018).

It is interesting to note that the noncumulative curves for the vulnerability process are symmetric in nature due to the fact that the vulnerability discovery

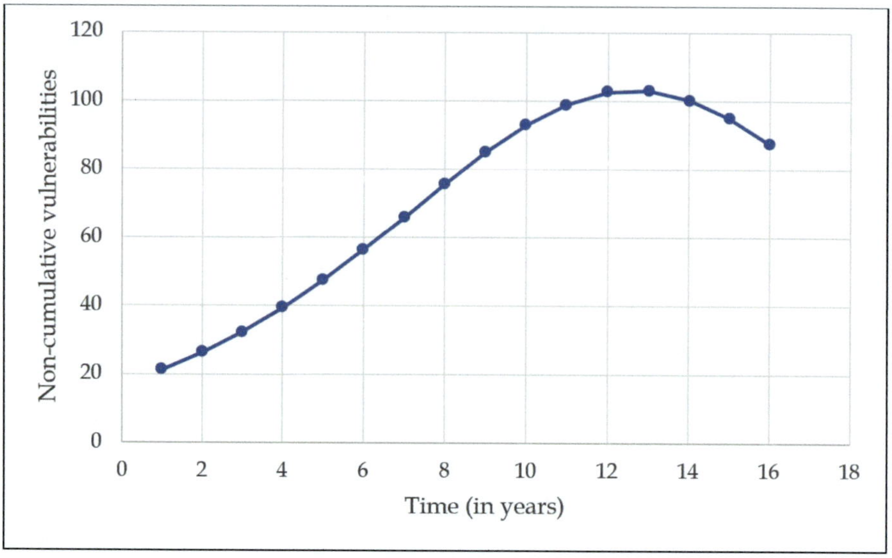

Figure 6.5 Noncumulative curve (Apple Mac OS X) (Source: Bhatt et al., 2018).

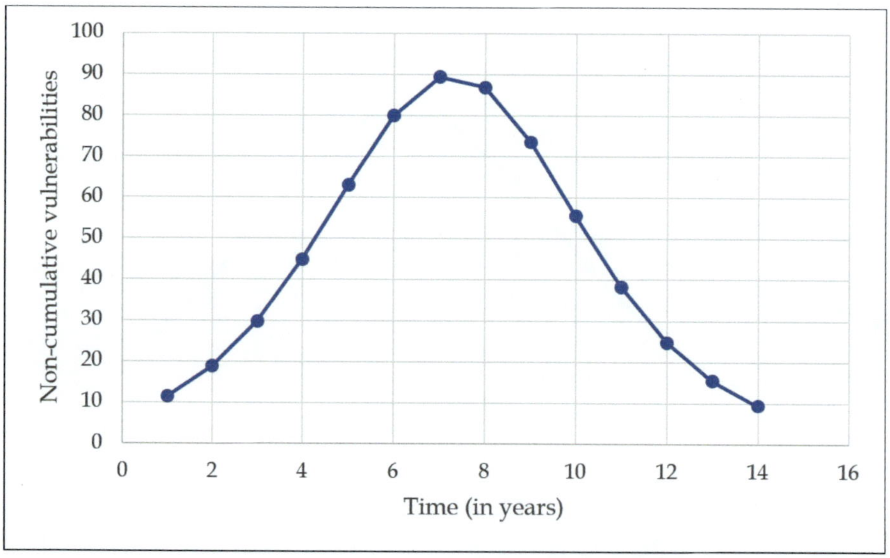

Figure 6.6 Noncumulative curve (Mac OS X Server) (Source: Bhatt et al., 2018).

function under consideration follows an S-shaped curve and its respective noncumulative vulnerability intensity curve is bell-shaped.

Table 6.6 Inflection points.

Time points	Dataset			
	Windows XP	Windows Server 2008	Apple Mac OS X	Apple Mac OS X Server
T_1	6.41	3.07	6.79	4.35
T^*	10.57	5.00	12.15	6.80
T_2	14.73	6.93	17.51	9.24

For the dataset of Windows XP, the time interval corresponding to $(0, T_1)$ impacts the discovery process with an increasing rate and constitutes those vulnerabilities that have a higher likelihood of discovery. In the time interval (T_1, T^*), due to the learning phenomenon in the S-shaped curve, the detectors understand the system and its market share also increases, implying a rapid discovery of many vulnerabilities. After attaining its peak at T^*, the discovery rate started to decrease and due to the symmetricity of the curve, an equal number of vulnerabilities are discovered that can be viewed in Table 6.7 for the categories V_2 and V_3. Availability of newer versions such as Windows Vista and Windows 7 influences the decrease of the instantaneous vulnerability rate. Finally, after time point T_2, the vulnerability discovery rate decreases due to the disinterest shown by the users in discovering the vulnerabilities. The vulnerabilities that are still present in the system and are not discovered even after the software support ended accounts in the category V_4. As in the case of Windows XP, the support ended in 2014, but some vulnerabilities are still present that were later discovered in the year 2017. The number of vulnerabilities in each category is calculated and given in Table 6.7.

Table 6.7 Number of vulnerabilities in each category.

Category	Dataset			
	Windows XP	Windows Server 2008	Apple Mac OS X	Apple Mac OS X Server
V_1	173	105	274	125
V_2	281	168	485	194
V_3	281	168	485	194
V_4	206	397	355	142

References

Alhazmi, O. H., & Malaiya, Y. K. (2005a). Modeling the vulnerability discovery process. *Proceedings of the 16th IEEE International Symposium on Software Reliability Engineering (ISSRE'05)* (pp. 129-138). Washington, DC, USA: IEEE Computer Society. Retrieved from https://www.cs.colostate.edu/~malaiya/pub/issre05.pdf

Aslam, T., Krsul, I., & Spafford, E. H. (1996). Use of a taxonomy of security faults.

Esser, S. (2004a). *Advisory 07/2004: CVS remote vulnerability*. Retrieved from lwn.net: https://lwn.net/Articles/85936/

Esser, S. (2004b). *Advisory 09/2004: More CVS remote vulnerabilities*. Retrieved from https://vulners.com/:https://vulners.com/securityvulns/SECURITYVULNS:DOC:6319

Gopalakrishna, R., & Spafford, E. H. (2005). *A Trend Analysis of Vulnerabilities*. West Lafayette, Indiana: CERIAS, Purdue University. Retrieved from https://www.cerias.purdue.edu/tools_and_resources/bibtex_archive/archive/2005-05.pdf

Kapur, P. K., & Garg, R. B. (1992). A software reliability growth model for an error-removal phenomenon. *Software Engineering Journal, 7*(4), 291-294.

Mac Os X Server. (2016). Retrieved from https://www.cvedetails.com/:https://www.cvedetails.com/product/2274/Apple-Mac-Os-X-Server.html

Mac Os X. (2016). Retrieved from https://www.cvedetails.com/:https://www.cvedetails.com/product/156/Apple-Mac-Os-X.html

Mahajan, V., Muller, E., & Srivastava, R. K. (1990). Determination of Adopter Categories by Using Innovation Diffusion Models. *Journal of Marketing Research, 27*(1), 37-50.

Ozment, A. (2007). Vulnerability Discovery & Software Security. *Ph.D. Dissertation*. Cambridge, UK.: University of Cambridge Computer Laboratory.

Windows Server 2008. (2016). Retrieved from cvedetails.com: https://www.cvedetails.com/product/11366/Microsoft-Windows-Server-2008.html

Windows Xp. (2016). Retrieved from https://www.cvedetails.com/:https://www.cvedetails.com/product/739/?q=Windows+Xp

Bhatt, N., Anand, A., Aggrawal, D., & Alhazmi, O. H. (2018). Categorization of vulnerabilities in a software. In *System Reliability Management* (pp. 121-135). CRC Press.

7

Multi-version VDMs

A software development company is compelled to produce newer versions of its products (i.e. computer programs, software, and so on) in order to keep up with the ever-increasing demands of both customers and suppliers in the market. Sharing the same source code across several software releases is the primary motivation for developing consecutive versions of software. This enables companies to do vulnerability and risk assessments both before and after the product is made available to the public. Because of the practice of sharing code between various releases, it is generally accepted that any number of security flaws found in the section of the code that is shared will be attributable to earlier versions of the software that includes the shared code. One of the most important presumptions is that the shared section of the code is tested while it is being used, even if the previous version of the software is no longer being utilized. The growing requirement for highly dependable software necessitates the development of a model that can estimate the number of vulnerabilities that are likely to be found in the course of their use. To achieve this objective, in this chapter, we discuss a detailed mathematical framework that can be used to address the requirement of designing safe software and offers an estimate of the number of vulnerabilities that can lead to a variety of gaps. In this chapter, we will investigate the key elements that might influence the process of discovering software vulnerabilities. Some of these aspects include the size and quantity of shared software code, the duration of the product's life cycle, and the frequency with which it is used.

7.1 Software Code

Many investigations have attempted to estimate fault prediction by analyzing software source code. The size and modularity of the source code can be determined by these criteria. However, in order to accurately forecast the finding of vulnerabilities in software with numerous versions, we need to investigate aspects such as shared source code, shared modularity, and similar functionality throughout the various versions. Here we outline some important aspects that the readers may consider to conceptualize multi-version modeling in VDMs.

7.1.1 Size of source code

As per the suggestions given by Akiyama (1971), the overall size of the software source code has a substantial correlation with the number of software errors. Ozment (2005), on the other hand, is of the opinion that as the vulnerability rates originating from extra software code are lower than in the original code, the number of vulnerabilities is not directly connected with the size of the source code. This is due to the fact that more software code is added. In other words, the structure of the program and the development strategy are connected to the density of software defects. Although these two points of view are alike, we shall adhere to both of them since they sufficiently describe software reliability growth modeling.

7.1.2 Software shared source code

The size of the software is one factor that may be used to estimate the amount of security flaws. For a single version of the software, the number of flaws has been found to have a direct correlation with the size of the program source code. On the other hand, shared code is the source of software vulnerabilities in various versions of software. According to Ozment (2005), the vulnerability density of extra software source code is lower than that of legacy code, while the code size of additional software source code is more than that of legacy code. Therefore, according to the notion of the software evolution model, shared source code is one of the most significant contributors to software vulnerability. When modeling the process of vulnerability detection for multi-version software, it is important to consider the influence that shared code has on the overall code size.

Given that a particular installed version of software is normally utilized until the introduction of a new version, its life span is contingent upon the plans of the software development team, which wish for the client to upgrade to the newer version. We can employ software market share information to find out when the usual software lifetime has come to an end in order to establish a typical software lifetime. The percentage of computers using Windows 98 fell once Windows XP was made available. At this time, Windows

98 has not reached the end of its useful life, and security flaws are still being discovered in it. Therefore, the software development policy is the primary factor that decides the influence of vulnerability detection rate from software lifetime.

7.2 Need for a Multiple-Version Software VDM

The discovery models that were discussed in the previous chapters just concentrates on standalone versions of software. A few of these models provide a responsible goodness-of-fit for the vast majority of software systems. However, the models do not provide an explanation for the anomalous increases in the vulnerability detection rate that may be attributed to the introduction of a new software version in a system that was previously running an older version of the software. Because of this oddity, we decided to look into a multiple-version software vulnerability discovery approach, which is abbreviated as MVDM. The ever-increasing demands placed on users and manufacturers alike have resulted in nearly all software now offering several versions that have been improved. As a direct consequence of this, numerous versions of software are being concurrently updated and used. It is anticipated that newer versions of software will have improved levels of both functionality and software dependability compared to earlier versions of software systems. Due to the fact that the software design is being altered or new code is being introduced, this gives birth to a vulnerability finding trend that is distinct from single-version VDMs. We may assume that shared features and code from older versions of the software may be subjected to testing during usage, despite the fact that the older version is not in widespread use any more. Also, during the testing of subsequent versions of software, previously unknown shared vulnerabilities in earlier versions of software are checked once again.

It is anticipated that newer versions of software will have improved levels of both software stability and functionality in comparison to earlier versions. Because of this, a vulnerability finding trend has emerged that is distinct from single-version VDM models like the AML model. This is due to the fact that the software design is frequently altered or new code is frequently added. In most cases, a considerable portion of the code or implementation from the prior version is passed down to the new version during the upgrade process. Even when the user base for a certain version may have drastically decreased, a component of its code may still be included in a more recent and widespread version. If an exploitable flaw is discovered in the shared code of the most recent version, it will also be present in all of the earlier versions that contain the same code.

It can be seen that vulnerability discovery rate shifts after each new version of software is released, and all previously used single vulnerability discovery models need to be taken into consideration. Here, we discuss a multi-version vulnerability discovery model that was proposed by Kim et.al. (2007) and Anand et.al. (2017).

7.3 Mathematical Model by Kim et al.

In order to appropriately estimate the number of vulnerabilities discovered in early versions of software, the shared vulnerability found in subsequent versions of software in the multiple version software vulnerability discovery modeling can be considered. In addition, we are operating under the assumption that shared vulnerabilities are the result of common functionality and source code. The subsequent version shares the functionality and code inherited from the previous version of the software.

When the second version rolls out, its rate of finding vulnerabilities increases along with the number of users and thus the rate of finding vulnerabilities in the first version decreases. To determine the prior vulnerability discovery rate, the vulnerability discovery rate should be calculated by summing it up.

The initial software vulnerability discovery model demonstrates the beginning of a saturation phase. However, the common vulnerabilities in the second version of the software cause the vulnerability discovery rate to increase once again, leading to a skewed logistic graph. The total number of vulnerabilities for a certain software, which has many versions, may be calculated by adding two terms together as follows:

$$\Omega(t) = \frac{N}{1 + NCe^{-rNt}} + \alpha \frac{N'}{1 + N'C'e^{-r'N'(t-\epsilon)}}. \tag{7.1}$$

Eqn (7.1) consists of two terms. The first term represents the first version of VDM, while the second term represents the vulnerability discovery in the second version. The parameter α represents common elements, such as shared code and shared functionality, whereas the parameter ϵ denotes the time difference between the release dates of the two versions.

The notion of modeling with two versions may be extended to encompass the modeling of software with many versions, as described in eqn (7.2)

$$\Omega(t) = \sum_{i=1}^{n} \alpha_i \frac{N_i}{1 + N_i C_i e^{-r_i N_i (t-\epsilon_i)}}. \tag{7.2}$$

7.4 Mathematical Model by Anand et al.

The increasing demand from customers and suppliers in the market compels a software development company to release consecutive iterations of its products (e.g. computer programs, software, etc.). The primary concept behind publishing consecutive versions is the sharing of code among multiple releases, which enables enterprises to evaluate the vulnerability and associated risk both before and following the software's release. Given the concept of code sharing over many releases, it is expected that the number of vulnerabilities found in the shared component of the code would be attributed to the older versions that include the shared code. One key assumption is that the section of code that is shared gets checked during usage, even if the earlier version is no longer being used. The urgent demand for highly dependable software necessitates a model that can forecast the likelihood of discovering vulnerabilities during usage. In pursuit of this objective, we can devise a mathematical model to address the vulnerabilities in different versions of software.

If there is just one version of the software available in the market, the potential vulnerabilities may be represented using the following model:

$$\Omega_1(t) = a_1 F_1(t), \tag{7.3}$$

where a_1 represents the potential number of vulnerabilities that can be exposed in the software, and $F_1(t)$ denotes the cumulative distribution function that represents the rate at which vulnerabilities will be detected and is given by $F_1(t) = \left(1 - \frac{(1+\beta_1)e^{-b_1 t}}{1+\beta_1 e^{-b_1 t}}\right)$.

The intense rivalry among enterprises necessitates the development of software versions in order to maintain their market position. Hence, it is conceivable that two distinct iterations of the software are concurrently available in the market. When new features are introduced to the software, it is possible that new vulnerabilities may arise, as well as vulnerabilities that might occur in the common code. These kinds of circumstances can be represented numerically as

$$\begin{aligned} \Omega_1(t) &= a_1 F_1(t) + a_1 (1 - F_1(t)) F_2(t - \tau_1) \\ \Omega_2(t) &= a_2 F_2(t - \tau_1), \end{aligned} \tag{7.4}$$

where a_2 represents the total number of vulnerabilities that can be identified in the second version and the term $F_2(t-\tau_1)$ follows a logistic distribution, i.e., $F_2(t-\tau_1)=\left(1-\frac{(1+\beta_2)e^{-b_2(t-\tau_1)}}{1+\beta_2 e^{-b_2(t-\tau_1)}}\right)$.

The vulnerability discovery phenomenon for the first version of software contains two components: the first component depicts the total number of vulnerabilities that were found in the first version, and the second component demonstrates the count of vulnerabilities that were found in the second version, but it is accounted for in the vulnerabilities that were found in the first version owing to code sharing. The number of vulnerabilities that are present in the second version is represented standalone in eqn (7.4).

When the software is updated with new functions for the second time, new lines of code are produced. This is because the software is being updated. This new code is included in the code that is already in place. There is a possibility that a vulnerability may be found in the newly introduced piece of the code, and at the same time, there is a possibility that some ambiguity could be found in the code that is shared by several users. The following equation provides a glimpse of vulnerabilities discovery pattern under three subsequent software versions.

$$\begin{aligned}\Omega_1(t) &= a_1F_1(t)+a_1(1-F_1(t))F_2(t-\tau_1)\\ &\qquad + a_1(1-F_1(t))(1-F_2(t-\tau_1))F_3(t-\tau_2)\\ \Omega_2(t) &= a_2F_2(t-\tau_1)+\ a_2(1-F_2(t-\tau_1))F_3(t-\tau_2)\\ \Omega_3(t) &= a_3F_3(t-\tau_2),\end{aligned} \tag{7.5}$$

where a_3 represents the total number of vulnerabilities that can be identified in the third version and the term $F_3(t-\tau_2)$ follows a logistic distribution, i.e., $F_2(t-\tau_2)=\left(1-\frac{(1+\beta_3)e^{-b_3(t-\tau_2)}}{1+\beta_3 e^{-b_3(t-\tau_2)}}\right)$.

Eqn (7.5) represents the sum of the vulnerabilities in the first version, along with the vulnerabilities revealed in the second and third versions. However, these vulnerabilities are attributed to the first version because of code sharing. Furthermore, the equation denotes the cumulative count of vulnerabilities in the second version, while the subsequent component indicates the number of flaws identified in the third version. However, these vulnerabilities are included in the total count of prior versions due to code sharing. Finally, it denotes the quantity of vulnerabilities contained in the third version.

The above-described model can also be generalized till *n* versions of the software as given in the following equation.

$$\begin{aligned}
\Omega_1(t) = a_1 F_1(t) + a_1(1 - F_1(t)) F_2(t - \tau_1) \\
+ a_1(1 - F_1(t))(1 - F_2(t - \tau_1)) F_3(t - \tau_2) + \ldots \\
+ a_1(1 - F_1(t)) \ldots F_n(t - \tau_{n-1}) \\
\Omega_2(t) = a_2 F_2(t - \tau_1) + a_2(1 - F_2(t - \tau_1)) F_3(t - \tau_2) \\
+ a_2(1 - F_2(t - \tau_1))(1 - F_3(t - \tau_2)) F_4(t - \tau_3) + \ldots \\
+ a_2(1 - F_2(t - \tau_1)) \ldots F_n(t - \tau_{n-1}) \\
\Omega_n(t) = a_n F_n(t - \tau_{n-1}).
\end{aligned} \tag{7.6}$$

References

Akiyama, F. (1971, August). An Example of Software System Debugging. In IFIP congress (1) (Vol. 71, pp. 353-359).

Kim, J., Malaiya, Y. K., & Ray, I. (2007). Vulnerability Discovery in Multi-Version Software Systems. *10th IEEE High Assurance Systems Engineering Symposium* (pp. 141-148). Plano, TX, USA: IEEE.

Anand, A., Das, S., Aggrawal, D., & Klochkov, Y. (2017). Vulnerability Discovery Modelling for Software with Multi-versions. In M. Ram, & J. P. Davim, *Advances in Reliability and System Engineering* (pp. 255-265). Cham: Springer.

8

Vulnerability Patching and its Extensions

The vulnerability discovery method (VDM) aims to predict the latent vulnerabilities that may be uncovered in a software after its release. Most vulnerabilities in software are often identified during the operating phase. The vulnerabilities identified in a software at any given time go through a lifespan, starting from their initial detection to their eventual resolution through patching. Optimally, VDMs are not employed for the purpose of identifying any susceptible module, but rather to evaluate the overall security architecture of a software system. Vulnerability analysis can aid software vendors in adopting a precise vulnerability discovery and management (VDM) approach to comprehend security patterns, allocate resources for patch and update creation, evaluate development plans, and bundle additional software with their own product.

The classification of VDMs is predicated on two classifications: a time-based modeling framework and an effort-based modeling framework. Time-based vulnerability discovery methods quantify the likelihood of identifying potential vulnerabilities at any given moment. The latter anticipates that the number of vulnerabilities will be assessed based on the level of effort exerted. The criteria used to estimate the vulnerability detection rate in majority of VDMs is governed by time. This chapter introduces a systematic strategy that may be used to estimate the number of fixes that need to be delivered, considering the vulnerabilities identified in a software system. The susceptibility patterns in a program have a substantial impact on the process of identifying vulnerabilities and then initiating the deployment of a patch to mitigate the potential risk of a breach. The integrated method emphasizes the connection between vulnerability patch modeling and the vulnerability finding phenomenon.

8.1 Modeling Software Patch Management

Once a software system is out in the market, it must address multiple security issues. In response, the company issues security patches to address the vulnerabilities identified in the software system. A vendor issues a fix exclusively when a vulnerability has been identified in a software. An essential factor in software maintenance is accurately predicting the number of patches that will be delivered to ensure stability. Vulnerability discovery models (VDMs) assist software vendors in recognizing security patterns, predicting security expenditures, and strategizing patch implementation. This chapter discusses new method that tackles the habit of sequentially developing patches in software based on the vendor or reporters identifying vulnerabilities. The susceptibility patterns in a program have a substantial impact on the process of identifying vulnerabilities and then initiating the deployment of a patch to mitigate the potential risk of a breach. In this chapter, we consider a mathematical framework to assess and direct the implementation of patches, considering the identified vulnerabilities. A model was developed by Anand et al. (2020) to address the functional relationship between the discovered vulnerabilities and the required number of patches to be published. This chapter specifically analyzes how the vulnerabilities disclosed to the vendor affect the process of deploying patches, based on the speed at which the underlying vulnerabilities are patched. The model enables a software vendor to evaluate security trends, determine the necessary allocation of resources for patch creation, and anticipate the number of patches to be distributed in accordance with the discovery of vulnerabilities. We assumed that a vendor is responsible for providing fixes to vulnerabilities that are reported directly by users, as well as addressing other problems that are found but not disclosed by users or are a result of faulty patches. The idea facilitates the understanding of the pattern in addressing vulnerabilities, whether it be influenced by previously resolved problems or by unsuccessful attempts at patching.

A similar study that was carried out by Arora *et al.* developed an analytical model that takes into consideration the chance of patching a software after it has been released on the market. The model revealed that disclosing a vulnerability prior to delivering a patch may lead to an increase in the number of attacks (Arora et al., 2006a). Providing updates at a later time may generate incentives for software vendors to grab the market, but it may also internalize customer loss when customers are exposed to a vulnerability that has not been patched. By leveraging externalities on patched users, August and Tunca investigated how the influences of an unpatched user can have an effect on the motivations of the vendor (August & Tunca, 2006). In addition, Arora *et al.* indicate that the fact that the patch was unavailable at the time of the disclosure indicated that there was an increase in the number of attacks. In their study, Arora and colleagues propose that a brief disclosure time could potentially have an impact on the patch deployment process, resulting in the rapid release of fixes (Arora et al., 2006b, Competitive and strategic effects in the timing of patch release, 2006b). Additionally, Arora *et al.* built a framework to investigate the best timing to disclose vulnerabilities as well as the patch distribution policies of the vendor (Arora, Nandkumar, & Telang, 2006). In their study, Temizkan *et al.* investigated the impact of a number of parameters that influence the release time of patches. The findings of their investigation recommended that vulnerabilities with high confidentiality or integrity should be patched early (Temizkan et al., 2012). Recent research conducted by Anand *et al.* has demonstrated the significance of patching and determining the most appropriate time to release a patch in order to reduce the number of system failures (Anand et al., 2016). Up until this point, Kansal *et al.* have made only a limited amount of effort to comprehend a software patch management process from a mathematical standpoint (Kansal et al., 2016).

The work addressed in this question that involved a mathematical framework to establish a correlation between the numbers of patches distributed owing to the impact of revealed vulnerabilities. In order to merge the technological relationship that exists between two or more systems, an approach to modeling that crosses disciplinary boundaries is discussed in this chapter. A vulnerability discovery phenomenon and a patch deployment procedure are the two processes that are included in the model that has been proposed. The process of patch deployment is a relationship between the number of patches that are going to be issued and the identification of vulnerabilities in a time horizon. Vulnerabilities that have been found are the real number of vulnerabilities for which patches are going to be provided. The release of these patches will be determined by the possibility that the software system will be affected. At the beginning of the process, we conduct an analysis of the phenomena of discovering vulnerabilities that are present in a software system. Consequently, we are able to solve the second stage in order to deduce the patch distribution procedure that caters to the vulnerabilities, which indicated a sequential creation of patches. The number of vulnerabilities that are found in a software is directly proportional to the rate at which fixes are distributed during the operational period of the software. It is essential that the behavior of the vulnerability discovery process be taken into consideration during the patch development process. Since the discovery process, which is advocated by Alhazmi and Malaiya, involves a multi-stage process for vulnerability discovery, the intensity function shows an increase during the early stage and then tails off. This is not because vulnerabilities are more difficult to find, but rather because there is a drop-in interest about a software version (Alhazmi & Malaiya, 2005a). The behavior of the discovery rate has a considerable influence on the patching process, and as a result, it was advised that we analyze the process together.

8.1.1 Assumptions

The mathematical model is built on the basis of the following assumptions:

- The software is subjected to being patched depending on the vulnerability that was discovered in the software.
- The non-homogeneous Poisson process (NHPP) is the trajectory that is anticipated to be followed by the vulnerability discovery phenomenon.
- The number of vulnerabilities that are discovered is directly proportional to the number of patches that actually get distributed.
- The phenomena of vulnerability discovery are a manifestation of the passage of time.
- In order to describe the learning effect of the vulnerabilities reporters, it is assumed that the vulnerability discovery rate is a nondecreasing S-shaped logistic function.
- There is a strong correlation between the time horizons for the vulnerabilities that were found and the patches that were implemented.

8.1.2 Notations

The following notations have been used in the chapter:

N: Total number of vulnerabilities present in a software.
A: Total number of patches to be deployed.
P, $P(t)$: Cumulative number of patches deployed in the time interval $(0, t]$.
Ω, $\Omega(t)$: Cumulative number of vulnerabilities discovered in the time interval $(0, t]$.
r: Vulnerability discovery rate.
s: Additional vulnerability discovery rate.
q_1: Rate of patching for vulnerabilities reported by users.
q_2: Rate of patching for additional vulnerabilities unreported by users.

8.2 Model Development

Quantitative measurements are taken by the modeling framework that was designed to determine the rate at which vulnerabilities are patched during the operational phase. Because of the fact that the updates are only applied after a vulnerability has been successfully identified. As a result of the fact that the purpose is to statistically evaluate the process of patch deployment for a software that is further dependent on the vulnerability discovery phenomenon, the vulnerability discovery is nevertheless dependent on the passage of time. Using the following functional form, the total number of patches that have been distributed at any given time point can be formulated as follows:

$$\frac{dP(t)}{dt} = \frac{dP(t)}{d\Omega(t)} \cdot \frac{d\Omega(t)}{dt}. \tag{8.1}$$

In eqn (8.1), the quantity of fixes issued at a given moment is contingent upon the quantity of vulnerabilities identified. Previous literature has not examined a method that quantitatively tracks the quantity of patches to be released according to the identified vulnerability pattern. Therefore, according to eqn (8.1), the functions P and Ω can be differentiated across time, but they are explicitly dependent on Ω and t, respectively. Below, a comprehensive analysis of each term present in eqn (8.1) is provided.

8.2.1 Modeling the numbers of patches with respect to vulnerabilities discovered

The software system is first published with a limited quantity of vulnerabilities that necessitate further patching. During its operating period, a software system allows for the deployment of many fixes within a specific timeframe to reduce risk. CERT and other organizations communicate with the vendor(s) to arrange the necessary patches within the specified timeframe. The initial element of eqn (8.1) pertains to the quantity of patches that have been issued as a result of identified vulnerabilities. According to Ozment (2007), the identification of a vulnerability can potentially lead to the identification of additional vulnerabilities that necessitate further patching. Two aspects have been considered when modeling the patching procedure at a specific time point. The quantity of patches to be issued at any given moment is directly proportional to the number of patches that need to be issued for the vulnerabilities that are being detected by the detectors. Additionally, as a result of the impact of previously addressed vulnerabilities, further patches are implemented in order to mitigate the risks associated with the newly identified vulnerabilities. The number of patches to be released for identified vulnerabilities depends on the rate of patching, which is influenced by the remaining number of patches to be released. Moreover, the rate of patching for newly encountered vulnerabilities can be aligned with the previously issued patches. The assumptions mentioned above can be quantitatively represented by the following differential equation:

$$\frac{dP(t)}{d\Omega(t)} = \left(q_1 + q_2\frac{P}{A}\right)(A - P). \tag{8.2}$$

The parameters q_1 and q_2 denote the distinct patching rates for identified vulnerabilities and the patching rates for newly identified vulnerabilities during the investigation of identified vulnerabilities and botched patches, respectively.

8.2.2 Modeling the number of vulnerabilities per unit time

The second component of eqn (8.1) denotes the vulnerability that has been identified at a specific moment in time. It has been postulated that the provision of patches is contingent upon the observed behavior of vulnerabilities. The model outlined in Chapter 3 has been employed to investigate the phenomenon of discovery. The phenomena of vulnerability detection have been classified into two categories: leading vulnerabilities and extra vulnerabilities, based on how they are reported to the vendor. In contrast to the primary vulnerabilities, supplementary vulnerabilities are detected as a result of the impact exerted by previously identified flaws. Upon the release of a software in the market, it is commonly considered that a significant number of the primary vulnerabilities are identified during the initial stages. Subsequently, as users gain knowledge about the software system, new vulnerabilities become apparent. The aforementioned vulnerability pattern can be mathematically represented by the following differential equation:

$$\frac{d\Omega(t)}{dt} = r(N - \Omega(t)) + s\frac{\Omega(t)}{N}(N - \Omega(t)). \tag{8.3}$$

The solution of the above differential eqn (8.3) considering the initial condition $\Omega(t = 0) = 0$ can be obtained as

$$\Omega(t) = N\left(\frac{1 - \exp(-(r + s)t)}{1 + (s/r)\exp(-(r + s)t)}\right). \tag{8.4}$$

Thus, eqn (8.4) can be used to find expected number of vulnerabilities discovered in a software at any time during the lifecycle of the software and can be given by

$$\frac{d\Omega(t)}{dt} = N\left(\frac{s(1 + (s/r))\exp(-(r + s)t)}{(1 + (s/r)\exp(-(r + s)t))^2}\right). \tag{8.5}$$

An observable pattern exhibited by the aforementioned model is that in the initial phases of a software release, the rate of vulnerability detection rises and reaches a peak, after which it begins to decline. As vulnerabilities are identified at a higher rate, the rate at which they are patched also increases, forming an S-shaped pattern. Over time, the patching process becomes less active as people lose interest in identifying vulnerabilities.

8.2.3 Formulation

To formulate the proposed model, the discussed components of eqn (8.1) to describe the patching rate under the influence of identified vulnerabilities have been combined. Substituting eqn (8.2) and (8.5) in eqn (8.1), the following expression can be obtained:

$$\frac{dP(t)}{dt} = N\left(q_1 + q_2\frac{P}{A}\right)(A-P)\frac{s\,(1+(s/r))\,exp\,(-\,(r+s)\,t)}{(1+(s/r)\,exp\,(-\,(r+s)\,t))^2}. \quad (8.6)$$

Eqn (8.6) can be further written as

$$\frac{dP(t)}{dt} = \eta\left(q_1 + q_2\frac{P}{A}\right)(A-P)\frac{\exp\,(-\,(r+s)\,t)}{(1+(s/r)\exp\,(-\,(r+s)\,t))^2}, \quad (8.7)$$

where $\eta = N \cdot s\,(1+(s/r))$.

Hence, the solution of eqn (8.7) describes the patch deployment phenomenon along with the vulnerability discovery during the operational phase. Solving eqn (8.7), the following expression can be obtained:

$$P\,(t) = A\left(\frac{1-\exp\,(-f(t))}{1+\frac{q_2}{q_1}\exp(-f(t))}\right), \quad (8.8)$$

where

$$f\,(t) = \eta\,(q_1+q_2)\frac{1-exp\,(-\,(r+s)\,t)}{1+(s/r)\,exp\,(-\,(r+s)\,t)}. \quad (8.9)$$

8.3 Numerical Illustration

This part provides a concise overview of the essential procedures involved in obtaining the data necessary for investigating the proposed modeling framework. Additionally, it outlines the process of conducting a quality analysis to assess the goodness of fit by calculating the parameters of the patch deployment model in order to get the best possible match with the observed samples.

8.3.1 Acquiring vulnerability and patch data

A multitude of repositories, including those managed by software vendors and third-party organizations, have been considered. The aforementioned repositories house advisory reports pertaining to the detected vulnerability, along with the corresponding patch specifics. Additionally, the data has been retrieved from the subsequent sources:

- A vendor advisory refers to a security report that is created by a software vendor to acknowledge the release of a fix in response to an identified vulnerability. Examples of security advisories include the Microsoft Security Bulletin (MS) and the Mozilla Firefox security advisory (MFSA).
- Third-party advisory refers to reports that are managed by providers external to the organization. For example, NVD and CVEDetails.

The vulnerability and patch datasets were obtained for the estimation purpose within the same timeframe. The data source CVEDetails was utilized to gather information on the vulnerabilities present in Microsoft products. MS bulletins are linked to each CVE entry. The patch data for each detected vulnerability for a specific time period has been analyzed by combining these data sources. The estimation of parameters for the mathematical model and validation with the real dataset using multiple goodness of fit criteria have been conducted using two Microsoft products, namely Windows 2000 and Windows XP. The data collection for Windows 2000 was obtained from the years 1999 to 2010. The Windows 2000 data collection was gathered between 1999 and 2010, comprising 194 updates addressing 490 vulnerabilities. In a similar vein, the dataset pertaining to Windows XP has a total of 319 updates addressing 588 vulnerabilities between the years 2000 and 2011.

8.3.2 Fitting the model to observed samples

The parameters of the VDM can be computed autonomously using the NLLS regression method, based on the vulnerability discovery data. Eqn (8.8) represents a comprehensive model that calculates the total number of vulnerabilities found in a software and the corresponding patches that need to be provided during its operational use. In order to estimate the parameter, it is possible to assume that the vulnerabilities identified are independent, and thereafter determine the corresponding number of patches. The estimation of the parameters of the vulnerability discovery model, namely *N*, *r*, and *s*, is facilitated by the utilization of eqn (8.4). Once the parameters have been calculated, they may be substituted into eqn (8.8) and the other parameters can be estimated using the regression approach. The parameters of the mathematical model can be determined using the SPSS software package.

In order to determine the statistical effectiveness of vulnerability patch modeling in fitting the observed sample of patches, it is necessary to examine the behavior of the vulnerability discovery function. Table 8.1 provides a description of the parameter estimations for the VDM. By substituting these estimates into eqn (8.8), we may estimate the VPM phenomena, which are presented in Table 8.2.

For Windows XP software, a significantly larger number of patches were provided as compared to the Windows 2000 dataset. This can be related to the increased prevalence of vulnerabilities in Windows XP. Furthermore, the rate at which the newly identified vulnerabilities are being fixed is higher than the rate at which the previously reported vulnerabilities are being fixed. The phenomenon of shared code can be ascribed to the analysis of vulnerabilities in software. When a vulnerability is identified for a specific software, its impact is also examined for other products within the same product line. In this scenario, the rate at which subsequent vulnerabilities are fixed has increased because it is influenced by the patches that were published to address vulnerabilities found in other software releases.

Table 8.1 Parameter estimates for VDM.

Parameters	Windows 2000	Windows XP
N	804.664	942.152
r	0.0312	0.0107
s	0.1638	0.3059

Table 8.2 Parameter estimates for VPM.

Parameters	Windows 2000	Windows XP
A	229.807	416.967
q_1	0.00012	0.0005
q_2	0.01292	0.0059

References

Alhazmi, O. H., & Malaiya, Y. K. (2005a). Modeling the vulnerability discovery process. *Proceedings of the 16th IEEE International Symposium on Software Reliability Engineering (ISSRE'05)* (pp. 129-138). Washington, DC, USA: IEEE Computer Society. Retrieved from https://www.cs.colostate.edu/~malaiya/pub/issre05.pdf

Anand, A., Agarwal, M., Tamura, Y., & Yamada, S. (2016). Economic impact of software patching and optimal release scheduling. *Quality and Reliability Engineering International, 33*(1), 149-157.

Anand, A., Kaur, J., & Inoue, S. (2020). Reliability modeling of multi-version software system incorporating the impact of infected patching. International Journal of Quality & Reliability Management, 37(6/7), 1071-1085.

Arora, A., Caulkins, J. P., & Telang, R. (2006a). Sell First, Fix Later: Impact of Patching on Software Quality. *Management Science, 52*(3), 465-471.

Arora, A., Forman, C. M., & Telang, R. (2006b). Competitive and strategic effects in the timing of patch release. *in fifth Workshop Econom. Inform. Security.* Cambridge, UK.

Arora, A., Nandkumar, A., & Telang, R. (2006c). Does information security attack frequency increase with vulnerability disclosure? An empirical analysis. *Information Systems Frontiers, 8*(5), 350-362

August, T., & Tunca, T. I. (2006). Network Software Security and User Incentives. *Management Science, 52*(11), 1703-1720.

Kansal, Y., Kumar, D., & Kapur, P. (2016). Vulnerability Patch Modeling. *International Journal of Reliability, Quality and Safety Engineering, 23*(6).

Temizkan, O., Kumar, R. L., Park, S., & Subramaniam, C. (2012). Patch Release Behaviors of Software Vendors in Response to Vulnerabilities: An Empirical Analysis. *Journal of Management Information Systems, 28*(4), 305-338.

Index

V

W

About the Authors

Dr. Adarsh Anand did his doctorate in the area of innovation diffusion modeling in marketing and software reliability assessment. Presently, he is working as an associate professor with the Department of Operational Research, University of Delhi, India. He has been conferred with Young Promising Researcher in the field of technology management and software reliability by the Society for Reliability Engineering, Quality and Operations Management (SREQOM) in 2012. He is a lifetime member of the Society for Reliability Engineering, Quality and Operations Management (SREQOM). He is also on the editorial board of *International Journal of System Assurance and Engineering Management* (Springer). He has guest edited several special issues for journals of international repute. He has edited two books, namely *System Reliability Management (Solutions and Technologies)* and *Recent Advancements in Software Reliability Assurance* under the banner of Taylor and Francis (CRC Press) and has authored one textbook, *Market Assessment with OR Applications*. He has recently edited another book, *Systems Performance Modeling*, with De Gruyter publishers. He has publications in journals of national and international repute. His research interest includes modeling innovation adoption and successive generations in marketing, software reliability growth modeling, and social media analysis.

Navneet Bhatt is an assistant professor with the Anil Surendra Modi School of Commerce at SVKM's Narsee Monjee Institute of Management Studies, Mumbai, India. He did his doctorate in the area of software vulnerability modeling from the University of Delhi, India. He is a lifetime member of the Society for Reliability Engineering, Quality and Operations Management (SREQOM). He has done six sigma green belt certifications from Indian Statistical Institute, Delhi. He has publications in journals of international repute. His research interest includes vulnerability discovery modeling, software reliability growth modeling, marketing management, and quality management.

Omar H. Alhazmi is a professor with the Department of Computer Science at Taibah University in Medina, Saudi Arabia. He received his Ph.D. in 2007 from Colorado State University, USA. Dr. Alhazmi has published over 50 articles in journals, conferences, and as book chapters in the areas of software vulnerabilities, security, reliability of software, and Internet of Things. He has also worked as a consultant to the e-government national program.